Role Play in the Early Years

The Toymaker's Workshop

and other stories

Jo Boulton and Judith Ackroyd

**Drama Activities
for 3–7 year olds:**

Book 3

David Fulton Publishers

For our friendship

David Fulton Publishers Ltd
The Chiswick Centre, 414 Chiswick High Road, London W4 5TF

www.fultonpublishers.co.uk

First published in Great Britain in 2004 by David Fulton Publishers

10 9 8 7 6 5 4 3 2 1

Note: The right of Jo Boulton and Judith Ackroyd to be identified as the authors of this work has been asserted by them in accordance with the Copyright, Designs and Patents Act 1988.

David Fulton Publishers is a division of Granada Learning Limited, part of ITV plc.

Copyright © Jo Boulton and Judith Ackroyd 2004

British Library Cataloguing in Publication Data
A catalogue record for this book is available from the British Library.

ISBN 1-84312-125-5

Typeset by FiSH Books, London
Printed and bound in Great Britain

Role Play in the Early Years

The
Toymaker's
Workshop
and other stories

Related titles of interest:

Drama Lessons for Five to Eleven-Year-Olds
Judith Ackroyd and Jo Boulton
1 85346 739 1

Beginning Drama 4–11, 2nd edition
Joe Winston and Miles Tandy
1 85346 702 2

Planning Children's Play and Learning in the Foundation Stage
Jane Drake
1 85346 752 9

Role Play in the Foundation Stage
Sue Rogers
1 85346 963 7

Outdoor Play in the Early Years
Helen Bilton
1 85346 952 1

Other titles in the series:

The Teddy Bears' Picnic and other stories
Jo Boulton and Judith Ackroyd
1 84312 123 9

Pirates and other adventures
Jo Boulton and Judith Ackroyd
1 84312 124 7

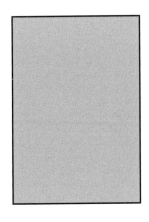

Contents

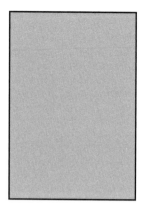

Acknowledgements

We would like to thank the students and teachers who have tried out these materials. We are especially grateful to Sue Gray, Estelle Crasto, Kate Ponté and Jane Lymn for their stories from the classroom. The support and friendship of colleagues in Education and Performance Studies at University College Northampton is valued and appreciated.

Over the years the work of Dorothy Heathcote, Gavin Bolton, Cecily O'Neill, David Davis and Jonothan Neelands has influenced our practice. We are grateful for their pioneering contributions to the field and their inspiration. Warm thanks to David Booth for his contagious enthusiasm for children's stories.

Thanks also to Nina Stibbe at David Fulton Publishers for asking us to write this series. We've loved the writing and the opportunity to work together again. We appreciate the enthusiasm and careful attention of Nina and her colleagues throughout the writing process.

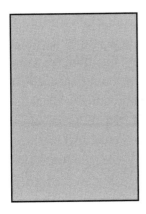

Introduction

There's something empowering for young children about drama.
It's about learning and problem-solving in their world.

We share teacher Angie Matthews' enthusiasm about using drama with young children and have therefore designed this series of three books to encourage a wider use of drama in early years settings. The series is designed to support those unfamiliar with drama activity as well as to offer experienced teachers a range of new materials.

Many teachers feel anxious about doing drama, but the fact is that teaching drama can no longer be avoided, no matter how scary it may seem. All children have a statutory entitlement to engage in dramatic activity. Drama is featured in the *Curriculum Guidance for the Foundation Stage* where children are required, for example, to *Use language to imagine and recreate roles and experiences* (DfEE/QCA, 2000: 58). Similarly in the National Curriculum, at Key Stage 1 drama activities are highlighted. For example, pupils must learn to

- use language and actions to explore and convey situations, characters and emotions;
- create and sustain roles individually and when working with others;
- comment constructively on drama they have watched or in which they have taken part.

(DfEE/QCA, 2000: 44)

The *National Literacy Strategy Framework for Teaching* makes explicit reference to drama. In Year 1 Term 1, for example, children will *re-enact stories in a variety of ways, e.g. through role play, using dolls or puppets* (DfEE, 1998: 20). Indeed, drama is an interactive and exciting teaching strategy which, by its very nature, illuminates the possibilities for interrelating the three language modes of speaking and listening, reading and writing.

While drama offers contexts and possibilities for development in aspects of English, it also provides a plethora of other learning opportunities at the same time. Thus while children are using persuasive language, they may also be considering the fragility of the environment. In addition, they may also be developing skills in group work and citizenship all at the same time – through involvement in the same one dramatic activity!

Many teachers are expected to use drama activities with little or no relevant training, often resulting in a lack of both confidence in and understanding of educational drama practice. Student teachers, early years practitioners in Foundation Stage settings and teachers in Key Stage 1 classrooms have regularly asked us for drama ideas they can try that will work with their children. The dramas in this series have been tried and tested by teachers new to drama and also by experienced practitioners. They have found these activities valuable in themselves and also useful as a springboard for developing their own ideas.

There is no doubt that early years practitioners recognise the pedagogic value of children's play. Home corners, imaginative play areas, pretend corners (call them what you will) have been a regular and exciting feature of the early years setting. There are a number of texts available offering ideas and advice on setting up such environments. The activities offered in this series, however, focus on ways that the adult can work in role alongside the children to enhance learning opportunities. Teacher involvement is crucial. Here it is not only the children who enter imaginative worlds but the children and their teacher who create and explore these fictional worlds together. This approach, namely the teacher in role, enables the teacher to work with the children from inside the drama. The teacher in role can structure the children's contributions, provide stimulating challenges and create appropriate atmospheres. The teacher in role creates situations that demand of the children particular language skills, understanding and empathy. The teacher in role provides a model of commitment to working in role that children can follow.

This book contains a range of drama teaching ideas organised into chapters. In each chapter two types of activity are presented. The drama activities are presented in the body of the page, and non-drama activities, such as reading or music, which are presented in circles. The layout of the activities offers practitioners the possibility of finding their own pathways through the material, appropriate to their own teaching context. This flexible approach enables pathways through the material to be selected according to a range of possible factors: the chosen learning objectives; knowledge of the children's needs; the space and time available; the level of teacher confidence, and perhaps the time of year or geographical locality or local events. The four teachers' stories of 'The Toymaker's Workshop', a drama from this book, demonstrate how they found their own pathways and different emphases. General aims for the chapters are provided, along with suggestions for resources. Each drama activity indicates possible teacher intentions to make clear the dramatic process. The relevance of each of the dramas to the National Curriculum and Early Learning Goals is set out at the end of the book.

In Book 1 of this series, *The Teddy Bears' Picnic and other stories*, we have included the transcript of a teaching session of 'The Park', a lesson in Book 1. This is not to invite you to replicate the way it was done in this instance, but to give you an idea of how drama occurs in the classroom as opposed to how it appears in a book. It illustrates how a teacher can respond to what the children bring and to the moments when they do not contribute. It is an honest, straightforward account of a drama-teaching experience with the words of both teacher and children.

The following chapters will help teachers to create a range of imaginary contexts in which children will encounter weird and wonderful, noble and naïve, wicked and whimsical characters.

Sarah Hudson taught her first ever drama lesson using one of these chapters. She writes:

Without wanting to sound too nauseating and over the top, I would say that this afternoon was one of the most rewarding I have had the pleasure of sharing with my class. It has definitely inspired me to continue to share drama activities with my class. If a novice, or definitely a non-expert, could manage this with such success, then I am sure anyone could.

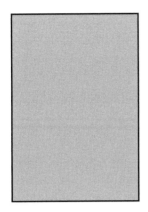

How to use this book

Where do I begin if I have never done drama before?

Looking at 'The Toymaker's Workshop' (Chapter 7) and then at 'Stories from the classroom' will give you a sense of how these dramas work and what is required of you. It is probably best to follow the activities step by step when you begin to use drama. You will soon want to add your own ideas. Book 1 of the series includes a transcript of a drama to get a feel of what might take place. It includes what was said by the children and teacher. Reading this may be helpful to those who are completely new to drama.

Do the dramas fulfil any National Curriculum objectives or Early Learning Goals?

Yes. All the dramas provide the possibility of covering a very wide range of Early Learning Goals (ELGs) and National Curriculum (NC) objectives, as you will see at the back of the book. You may choose to focus on specific objectives which may be most appropriate to your children and their needs.

How many children do I work with?

These dramas have been designed for use with any number of children between groups of four and thirty.

How long do the dramas take?

You need to consider how long you have and how long you wish to give to the activities. We recommend a maximum of thirty minutes with children in the Foundation Stage. However, we have sometimes lost track of time and found that we have been working for much longer. You need to gauge the children's response.

You may choose to teach just one activity and then pick up the story again another time. You can do a drama in one session or over a week.

What initial information is provided?

- Each chapter is laid out with an introduction telling the story of the drama.
- The overall aims of the drama are provided which concern both drama and other curriculum areas.
- Key themes are listed.

- Resources are listed. These are usually optional, but any essential items are indicated. Some resources have been included, such as the words to the 'Humpty Dumpty' song.
- Also provided are suggestions for imaginative play areas.

How are the activities explained?

- Drama and non-drama activities are provided. The non-drama activities are presented in circles at the side of the page.
- Teacher's intentions for each activity are listed. These pertain to the thinking behind the particular activity described. Headings provide an indication of both the type of dramatic activity (e.g. 'Still image') and the content (e.g. 'Looking around the workshop').
- *Italics* are used to distinguish direct speech and explanation. The direct speech provides suggestions of what the teacher might say and examples of what children have said during the drama.
- Clear explanations of drama terminology used in the chapters are included in the 'Glossary'.
- A number of generic games used in the dramas are also described in detail.

Do I have to follow the whole plan?

No. It is important that you read through the materials to familiarise yourself with the story. You can then make choices about your own pathway through the materials. In the 'Stories from the classroom' we see that Jane did choose to follow the plan, while Sue chose to do some additional movement activities when teaching 'The Toymaker's Workshop' and Kate added a thought tunnel for Charlie Bear. Estelle chose to focus on the still image work and dramatic play activities with her class. The plans can be followed as they are laid out, or you can select which activities you wish to use depending on your experience, your context and your children. You can make the dramas your own as Sue, Estelle, Jane and Kate have done.

Do I have to use teacher in role?

Yes. All of these dramas include teacher in role to some degree. The rationale behind this series of books is based upon the teacher working in role from inside the fiction alongside the children. However, this does not mean that you have to use exaggerated voices and walks. You are not required to wear a costume or use props, although we provide suggestions of what might be used to help young children distinguish between you as teacher and you in role. It is important that you make it very clear when you are in role to avoid confusion. A hat is often easy to put on and take off as you move between teacher and role.

How do I use an imaginative play area?

Imaginative play areas can be set up by the teacher and children together. They provide a context for the dramas. This does not mean to say that you have to do the drama in the imaginative play area. If you are working with a large group, there won't be room. In this case, you can refer to the imaginative play area as if it is your backdrop. Suggestions for how you might create such areas are provided in the chapters. All the dramas may be taught without imaginative play areas. If you are working in a large space, such as a school hall, we strongly recommend that a corner is cordoned off, since too much space can lead to difficulties.

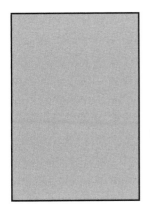

Stories from the classroom

The Toymaker's Workshop

We asked some local teachers to write stories about their experiences of 'The Toymaker's Workshop' (Chapter 7) with their classes. Sue Gray is in her first year of teaching. She is an English specialist with a little experience of drama. She is not very confident about using teacher in role but is quickly becoming more confident the more she uses it! Her class of seventeen reception children includes seven with speech difficulties. Estelle Crasto is a third-year BAQTS student who is just about to undertake her final school experience. She had met her class only two days before she taught the drama session with them. Estelle is a maths specialist with only six hours of drama training within her core English sessions. She is, however, very keen to use drama in her teaching to inspire the children. Kate Ponté is also a final-year BAQTS student but she is an English specialist who has had some extra drama training on her specialism course. Jane Lymn is a second-year BAQTS English specialist on a school placement in a village primary school.

▮ Sue Gray's story
▮ Rowlett Primary School, Corby, Northamptonshire

The context of our work was: approaching Christmas (and all that that entails!); on one child's birthday; in the classroom; Monday morning.

We began the activity with a 'circle' discussion about toys. This was particularly good, as it was one child's birthday and he was keen to talk about the toys he had received, which encouraged the other children to talk about toys they had received on their birthdays.

Although, as with most Foundation Stage classes, we carry out a lot of informal drama through role play and plenaries, this activity, using a more formal approach of teacher in role (TIR), was relatively new to the children. I was unsure of how they would react to my being in role as 'Tonica the Toymaker'. In fact most of them coped very well, soon becoming drawn into the roles of Tonica's helpers.

After explaining the signals to the children of teacher in role (wearing a headscarf and overall when I was in role), I took them around the different areas of 'my workshop', explaining which part we were in and allowing the children to lead the discussion with regard to the materials and toys they could 'see'. I was amazed to find that we made huge glass giraffes among other things!

As we passed from area to area, the children chose where they would like to work and began to carry out their chosen tasks in role. This was fantastic, as it was easy to distinguish the 'stuffers' from the 'menders' by their actions. It was also wonderful to see them building the 'toys' together, helping each other to 'see' what they saw. What was particularly gratifying, however, was the way that children with very poor speech were able to take part in the activity equally, and with obvious enjoyment.

Most of the children were very enthusiastic and adapted well to using their imagination. Others, however, sought items within the classroom, such as 'Stickle Bricks' and 'Mobilo', and began to make toys with them, appearing to need to work in a more concrete, rather than an abstract way. Although this was not my intention, I realised (too late) that I had not explained clearly enough that they were to work entirely with their imagination. However, the work was of value, as the children were still working cooperatively to produce toys, which was the intention. When carrying out such an activity again, I will explain the objectives more carefully, in order to encourage the children to use the full range of resources that their imagination can provide.

With hindsight, I would definitely collect a range of toys to show the children as a stimulus for discussion, particularly more traditional toys and toys made from different materials. Many of the children were fixed on 'Action Man' and 'Barbie' and the accompanying paraphernalia, demonstrating limited experience of a range of toys.

The children appeared to enjoy the activity immensely, as did I! We continued to use it as part of our physical development the following day, when we became the toys and began to explore different ways of moving around the room. As part of our work in creative development later in the week, we made toys from 'junk' materials.

One of the main benefits, apart from its scope across the Foundation Stage curriculum, was the ability to engage all of the children in my class. I have some children who articulate poorly. They can sometimes be excluded from more speech-based activities. It was clear that the activities allowed them to achieve on an equal basis with the more able speakers. A really inclusive and fun activity!

▮ Estelle Crasto's story
▮ St Mary's Catholic Primary School, Northampton

This was a short session of forty minutes with a Year Two class of twenty-four children. Since it was a one-day visit leading up to my final teaching practice, the children were not that familiar with me and we had not seen each other for a week – they were still trying to master my name! The class had been working on the cross-curricular theme of toys for a while and had constructed a toyshop imaginative play area which was about to be taken down and changed into something else. I decided to make the most of this.

I had set up the classroom and moved the tables, only to be told that the violin lessons were taking place in our class and we were going to be in the hall! The school was being extended so, between that and wet play, being flexible was paramount.

I decided to start with the 'Circles' discussion activity because the class was not brilliant at turn taking on the carpet. I wrapped a box in gold paper and we passed it around, using the standard rules for any circle-time activity. It was not long since Christmas, so I thought they would be keen to tell me what they had received from Santa, and where and why we buy presents. However, it was like pulling teeth! Normally they hardly stop to draw breath and then, when they had everyone's undivided attention, they could barely manage a whisper. A few responded with 'Barbie' and 'PlayStation' games. I asked them what type of present they would buy for their best friend and why. Some were slightly more imaginative: 'a magic set' and 'climbing frame' were offered. At the end I realised that I should have begun with the more able children, even though I knew that most of the children had good oracy skills in class when chatting to friends. Next time I would begin with an activity that would help them feel more at ease.

I continued with the main activities – and what a difference! The children became animated and almost all of them put their hands up to tell Tonica of their great ideas for toys that could be made at the toy shop. These included a suit of armour – made out of plastic, and a bicycle and a boat – with lots of detail about how it would work. When I asked one child, for a second time, what he could make, half the class shouted out, *'That's not fair, he's had a turn!'* They were so engaged with the activity that the 'still image' work and 'dramatic play' followed quite naturally.

I enjoyed watching their responses so much that I forgot to look at the clock, and it all came to an abrupt end, since the hall was needed for lunch.

'You were Tonica really, weren't you Mrs Crasto?' was one child's parting comment as we reached the classroom door.

Kate Ponté's story
Ecton Brook Primary School, Northampton

On my final third-year placement at Ecton Brook Primary School, I have a mixed Year 1 and 2 class. There are twenty-nine children in the class of very mixed ability including children with special educational needs, children with challenging behaviour and children with English as an additional language. I planned to teach two lessons of forty minutes each on two consecutive Thursdays. Unfortunately on the second Thursday it snowed, and the school was closed. 'Snowday' meant we revisited the toymaker's workshop two weeks later.

Session 1

The session introduction included a general chat about drama since the children had little previous experience. I wanted to encourage them to forget about classroom normalities such as putting up one's hand to speak. I wanted them to think about drama as something new altogether. I set the scene using the instructions in the lesson plan:
   'We are going to tell a story about the toyshop today. Will you help me?'

The children seemed excited and full of enthusiasm when I asked them:
   'Would you like to be the people who help Tonica the toymaker?
   I am going to be Tonica the toymaker now. I'll walk in and start to talk to you.'

As soon as I walked in 'in role' there were a lot of giggles as the children accepted the situation.

During the discussion about what we should make at the workshop, Jay and Rhys, who had never spoken to me before, could not stop! They were full of ideas about what they could make and what they would need. Jay was keen to make old-fashioned wooden toys, and she needed wood and paint, and of course electricity for her tools. The next activity was the still image. I told the children to be soldiers and dolls to start with to help include every-one. Then I asked the children to be a toy of their choice. *No one* was lost for an idea. There were some lovely suggestions: skeletons, teddy bears having a picnic, and puppets. It was a dull day, and when I turned the lights off to make the workshop come to life, it made a real difference in the classroom. The toys came alive beautifully and I was able to move among them and talk to them. Then I turned on the lights and all the children fell silent while they whisked back to their original positions. We did it again and again at the children's request, well into the lunch break.

Session 2

This involved meeting Charlie Bear. The biggest surprise to me in this session was Connor, who had always struck me as the class thug. Children always seemed to be left crying in his wake as a result of his physical and mental strength of character. Connor's contribution to the hot seat was to *'make Charlie into a brand new golden bear that everyone would want to take care of and play with'*. It was a real gem. The apprentice scenario offered many opportunities for discussion and description of what the children were making and how they were doing it. Things were *'plastic, metal, bent, moulded and heated'*. *'Put a hole in it!'* *'We're making pull along toys.'* *'Ours are African figures and wooden donkeys.'*

Finally, I decided to slip in a thought tunnel for Charlie Bear. This wasn't in the plan but I wanted the children to be able to get inside Charlie's head. This went really well, with the children showing real sensitivity. The plenary provided a perfect opportunity to recount the story and think about the characters we had met.

The children have been asking me to do drama again and again, and I am planning at least one drama session in each week of my block placement. This was a really good lesson, and I enjoyed teaching it as much as the children enjoyed being involved.

▌Jane Lymn's story
▌Wilby C of E Primary School, Wilby, Northamptonshire

I am in my second year of teacher training. Never having had direct involvement in teaching drama or 'being in role', I was a little anxious about trying drama with my class of thirty mixed Year 1 and 2 children who were very lively and had had little experience of drama themselves. I was unsure how they would react to me in role. The drama was taught over four days in the final week of my placement.

Day 1
Introducing Tonica's toy workshop

I began by explaining some of the drama conventions we would be using (teacher in role, children in role, improvisation, still images). We sat in a circle and I ' became' Tonica. I had read through the material several times but still felt I needed some notes for reference, so the clipboard was a handy prop. Looking back, I would have liked to have had the confidence to go in without notes.

The children's reactions to me in role were varied. Some immediately became involved and addressed me as 'Tonica'. Others found it a lot harder and giggled, and clearly felt inhibited to begin with. In this session the children in role as toyshop workers talked about the toys they would make. This did not take as long as expected, so I filled the gap by asking them to demonstrate how they would make their toys. A few children took this opportunity to charge around the hall being aeroplanes or racing cars. My dilemma was how to calm things down without going back to 'teacher mode', so in role as Tonica I called the workers together to explain the criteria for giving them a job. This worked well.

Day 2
Discovering what's in the workshop

The children were keen to begin after the previous day's session. I reinforced the concept of still image before going into role. This worked really well. When I introduced the magic element of the toys coming alive, I decided to adopt a signal for them to move about. I told them that when the lights went out at the end of the day the toys came alive. As I turned the lights out and pretended to go home, some of the children ran around shouting. After a few seconds (and resisting the temptation of teacher mode again), I turned the lights back on and became Tonica coming back to work the next day. Once the children had returned to their places and were quiet, I told them that the Police had called me in the night because there had been some complaints about noise in the workshop. I said I hoped I would not be disturbed again tonight. As I turned the lights off the children became the toys again and moved around very quietly.

Day 3
Meeting Charlie the Bear

Most of the children's reactions were amazing. This was their chance to ask questions, offer help and make suggestions, which they did very convincingly. I explained Charlie's dilemma and emphasised that he would be very nervous and even a little afraid of them. As I entered the room as Charlie Bear, wearing a very old sheepskin coat inside out, some children began to laugh loudly. I began to shrink back and tried to leave the room when two Year 1 boys told the class to *'Be quiet, he's scared'*. The class calmed down and I sat in the circle with them. The same two boys immediately came over, rubbed my arms and told me not to be afraid. Other children joined in and suggested ways they could help me: *'We could wash you and mend your ear.' 'We could give you a new squeaker.' 'We could find you a new home.'* Most of the class was completely absorbed.

Day 4
A new challenge for the apprentices.

By now the children were getting really involved and were asking me during the morning, *'Is there another visitor coming to the workshop? Who will it be?'* I introduced Rupert and the children went straight into role. They had completely taken ownership of the toyshop and had lots of enthusiasm for the task of completing the toy orders in Tonica's absence. They were listening intently to Rupert's instructions, and they all came up with suggestions for toys and expressed their confidence to complete the task.

Lots of children said how much they had enjoyed the drama and I was surprised how much I had enjoyed it too. I can now look forward to the next time with increased confidence.

The Lonely Dragon

There is a cave halfway up the mountain where a dragon lives. The villagers who live at the bottom of the mountain are not happy about the dragon and hide whenever they see him coming. One day they see him crying and decide to find out why he is so sad. The villagers find out about the dragon and befriend him.

Aims

- To explore differences between people.
- To discuss the danger of jumping to conclusions about people.
- To work together to solve problems.

Themes

- Dragons.
- Fear of the unknown.
- Friendship.
- Loneliness.
- Being misunderstood.

Resources

Optional: A large piece of 'dragon-coloured' material.
Large sheets of paper and pens.

The imaginative play area can be designed as a cave, a village green or a park.

Notes

The idea for this drama came originally from a book called *The Dragon Who Couldn't Help Breathing Fire* by Denis Bond. In this story the dragon's problem is that he breathes fire when he laughs and causes havoc wherever he goes. He eventually finds that he can be useful to people by lighting fires for them. This drama takes on the spirit of the story.

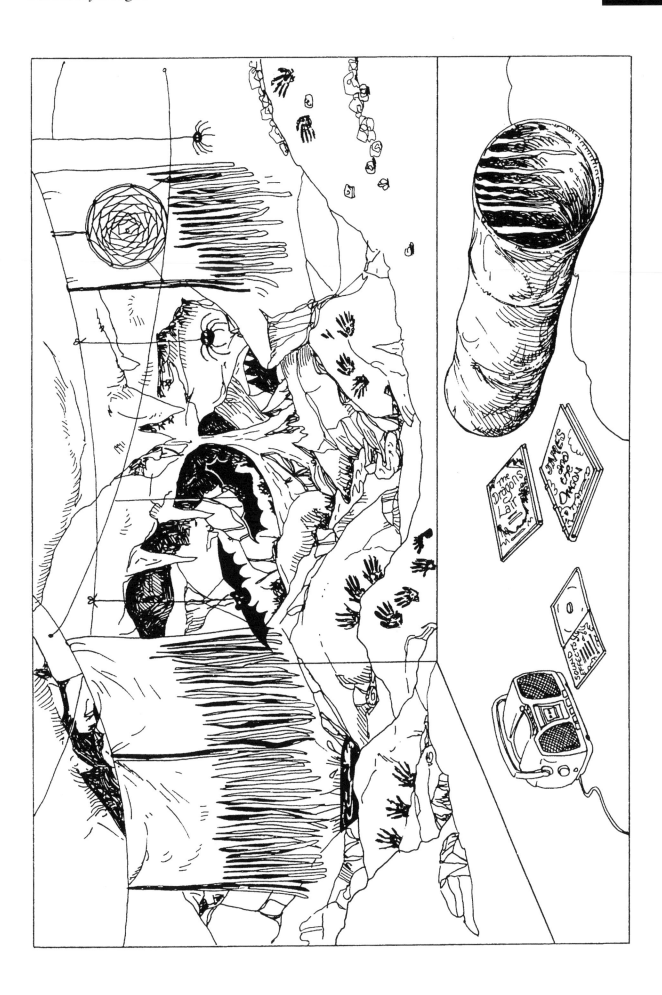

Activity 1   The villagers live in fear

Teacher's intentions

- To build belief in the setting.
- To introduce the dragon as a threat to the village.
- To tell the beginning of the story collectively, using the children's ideas.

Discussion and narration: setting the scene

Tell the children that you are going to tell a story about a village which is situated at the bottom of a mountain. Ask the children to imagine what things they would see if they walked through the village. Would there be a park, a river, shops? Try to build up a clear picture of the village using words. Tell the beginning of the story:

Halfway up the mountain was a cave and in the cave lived a dragon. No one in the village liked the dragon. No one ever went up the mountain to see him. In fact he never ever had any visitors.

Ask the children why no one ever visited the dragon. They may say things like:

- *He would eat them.*
- *He is frightening.*
- *He has big claws and might scratch them.*
- *He breathes fire.*

Whatever they suggest, try to emphasise that no one has ever seen him do any of the bad things they are worried about. Lead a storytelling session, encouraging the children to fill in the details.

- *The people in the village were afraid of the dragon because they thought he might . . .*
- *They believed he would . . .*
- *They were afraid he was going to . . .*

Finish with:

- *They never saw him do any of these things, but they were always afraid he would.*

Stories and poems

Read stories and poems about dragons.

Activity 2 How do we feel when we see the dragon?

Teacher's intentions

- To continue to build belief in the village, and the threat felt by the villagers.
- To bring the village to life.
- To explore the feelings of the villagers.

Still images: when the dragon comes

Tell the children that the dragon never comes very close to the people but he will sometimes be seen flying overhead and watching them. Ask the children to work in groups to produce a still image or picture of something that is happening in the village one sunny day. Brainstorm a few ideas first to make sure everyone has an idea of what they might be doing (e.g. playing football, going shopping, having a picnic by the river). Practise the images, remembering that people in still pictures can't move or talk! Look at the images one at a time. Try to guess what is going on in each picture. You are able to talk to the people in the image by touching them on the shoulder. Perhaps ask basic questions at first such as:

- *What are you doing?*
- *Who are you with?*
- *What are you holding in your hand?*
- *What's the weather like today?*

Ask the children to go back to their original images and then imagine how the picture would change if the dragon was to be seen flying towards them. Ask them to practise changing the image from one to the other. Look at each group in turn showing these two linked images. Again, it is possible to talk to the people in the picture by touching them on the shoulder. Ask questions such as:

- *What can you see?*
- *Tell me what it looks like.*
- *What can you hear?*
- *How do you feel?*
- *Why are you looking so frightened?*
- *What are you going to do now?*
- *What do you think the dragon might do?*

Collective drawing

The whole class can sit in a circle around a large sheet of paper and come forward one at a time to contribute to part of a drawing of a dragon. Individuals choose which part of the dragon they would like to draw and the colours to use. The finished dragon will be an exciting mix of the children's collective ideas. This could be done in groups rather than with the whole class.

Music and movement

Make dragon music using different instruments. You could try to make sounds such as the dragon's wings flapping, the dragon roaring, the dragon walking, the dragon breathing fire. Different movements could be added to the music.

Write a list

Decide on all the things that need to be done to prepare for the event. Write a list and choose which activity children will be involved in.

Activity 3   The village gathers for a celebration

Teacher's intentions

- To introduce sympathy for the dragon.
- To allow for group decision-making.
- To provide opportunity for interaction between characters.

Improvisation: the great event is planned

Tell the children that there is going to be a big event happening on the village green that afternoon or evening. It could be linked in with a particular time of year if appropriate, such as bonfire night, summer fair, Diwali or May Day. Ask the children to suggest what could be happening and come to a collective decision. Ask the children to think of what would need to be prepared and organised for the event (e.g. food, decorations, entertainment). Tell the children that they are going to be working in the space which is the village green and that when you want them to stop working you will give a signal such as calling 'Three, two, one, Freeze'. Make sure all the children are aware of the signal before starting the improvisation. Children can work individually, in pairs or in small groups to get everything ready. The teacher can join in, in role as a villager, helping out where necessary with ideas and advice. Allow this to go on for as long as the children are engaged – this may be five or fifteen minutes! Give the agreed signal 'Three, two, one, Freeze'. When the children are frozen in time continue the story:

Shared writing of a poster

Group or whole class shared writing of a poster advertising the village event.

As everyone was busy suddenly in the distance they saw the dragon flying slowly towards them. As they stood looking at the dragon they were utterly amazed to see tears rolling down his cheeks. He turned round and flew silently back to his cave.

Discussion in role: what could be wrong with the dragon?

Ask the children to sit down. Still in role, begin to talk about what they have just seen.

Some may feel immediate sympathy for the poor dragon, others may be suspicious. Encourage discussion.

- *Did you see the dragon just now?*
- *Why do you think he was crying?*
- *He might just be tricking us.*
- *What do you think we should do?*
- *I feel bad about him, he looked so lonely.*

The children usually decide to send some people to visit the dragon in his cave to find out what is the matter. It is better from an organisational and classroom management point of view if all the villagers go. However, if only some of them volunteer you may decide to allow the others to watch the proceedings and report back once they have visited the dragon. Alternatively, the children may decide to send the dragon a letter or an invitation, but there is the problem that perhaps he can't read. Decide what needs to be said to the dragon and what questions they want answered.

Activity 4   The journey to the dragon's cave

Teacher's intentions

- To represent the journey using movement and description.
- To add anticipation and tension to the story.

Dramatic construction and word collage: the path up the mountain

Explain to the children that they are going to represent the path up the mountain to the dragon's cave. Ask them to stand in two lines facing each other. They can bend the lines slightly to indicate the twists and turns in a real mountain path. Ask them to think of a physical object that they might see along that path (e.g. a tree, a bush, a rock, a stream). Ask the children to stand in a way that represents that object (e.g. crouched down for a rock, arms outstretched for a tree). Ask them to think of a word or words to describe themselves. Depending on the age of the children you could make this instruction more specific (e.g. think of three adjectives or verbs to describe what you are without using the noun itself: *tall, leafy, swaying*). Walk along the path pausing in front of each object and hear the children speak their words. You can also give precise instructions as to how the words are to be spoken (e.g. everyone whisper their words), or you could ask them to think about how to say their words depending on what they are representing (e.g. shouting *Cold, Hard, Grey* [a rock] or whispering *soft, white, dancing* [flowers]. This journey can be repeated a number of times in different ways to create word collages.

> **Collect...**
> Pictures of different dragons.

> **Brainstorm happy and sad words**
> Think about words to describe the dragon at different points in the story. How did he feel when he flew towards the villagers? How did he feel at the end?

The dragon, by Charlie

Write an invitation

Shared or individual writing of an invitation to send or give to the dragon.

Activity 5 Meeting the dragon

Teacher's intentions

- To introduce the teacher in role.
- To ask and answer questions in role.
- To begin to explore misunderstandings and assumptions made about others.

Narration: the journey ends

Set up a chair which will be inside the dragon's cave. It adds atmosphere if the chair is covered in an appropriately coloured drape. Ask the children to sit outside the cave as if they have just arrived after their journey. Narrate:

After a difficult climb up the mountain past rocks and streams, trees and bushes, the villagers arrived at the dragon's cave. As they sat and waited they could hear a noise coming from inside the cave.

Sit on the chair and show through your body language and facial expression that you are not happy! Perhaps sniff loudly or blow your nose.

Hello? Is there anyone there? I can hear someone outside the cave. Don't hurt me.

Art and literacy

Individual paintings, drawings or collages of dragons. Decide on a name for the dragon.

Draw the children into conversation. The dragon is very lonely and has no friends. People are afraid of dragons because of stories which aren't always true. He has never eaten anyone and is a vegetarian who prefers the carrots he grows in his garden. No one ever speaks to him in the village and they always look frightened. He can't help looking scary. It's the way he was born. He only breathes fire when he laughs.

Hopefully the children will discuss their fears and realise they have no foundation. They often invite the dragon to come down to the village to join in the celebrations. The dragon takes advice about what to wear, and the children can discuss health and safety issues with him about the possibility of his breathing fire.

Activity 6   The celebration!

Teacher's intention

- To see the situation from another's viewpoint.

Thought tunnel: the dragon walks down the mountain

Ask the children to re-create the path down the mountain. However, this time ask them to imagine how the dragon might be feeling as he walks slowly towards the village green. What are the thoughts going round in his head? As you walk past each one, pause so they can speak aloud what they imagine the dragon might be thinking:

- *I'm really excited.*
- *I hope they'll be nice to me.*
- *Perhaps it's a trick and they're going to kill me.*
- *I hope I don't knock anyone over with my tail.*

As you arrive at the end of the thought tunnel, turn around slowly and address the children as if they were the villagers:

Hello everyone. Thank you for inviting me. Is there anything I can do to help?

It may be suggested that the dragon helps to put up the balloons or even to light the bonfire or barbecue. The dragon will have to explain that he can't breathe fire unless someone makes him laugh. The villagers think of ways, such as pulling funny faces, telling jokes and tickling him with a feather. The dragon can decide what makes him laugh. The ending of the drama can be improvised or narrated:

The celebration went with a swing. Everyone enjoyed it, especially the dragon. From that day to this the people in the village have not been afraid of the dragon because they now know him and know that although he looks strange and different he is really a friendly dragon after all.

Plenary discussion

- Why was the dragon lonely?
- How did the villagers feel about him at the beginning of the story?
- What happened to change their minds?

Speech and thought bubbles

What is the dragon thinking and feeling at different points in the story? Draw speech and thought bubbles. What he says and what he thinks may of course be different.

Writing poetry

The words used in the word collage may be collected and written as a shared poem.

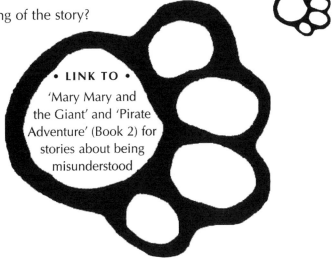

• LINK TO •
'Mary Mary and the Giant' and 'Pirate Adventure' (Book 2) for stories about being misunderstood

2 Off to Market

The children create a market scene, a duologue and a sound collage of market sounds. Their market-day is interrupted by the arrival of a stranger in vibrant clothes, pulling a colourful wagon with bells on its wheels. He, too, has a market stall and the goods are in his wagon. He promises that the goods are all magic. Should the children believe him and ask him to show them his wares?

Aims

- To develop the imagination.
- To use repetition to familiarise children with a few written words.
- To use the voice with a degree of control.
- To offer a view that things which look dull may not be.

Themes

- Markets.
- Trust.
- Judging people by first impressions.

Resources

Optional: Colourful bag and/or coat.

The imaginative play area can be the market.

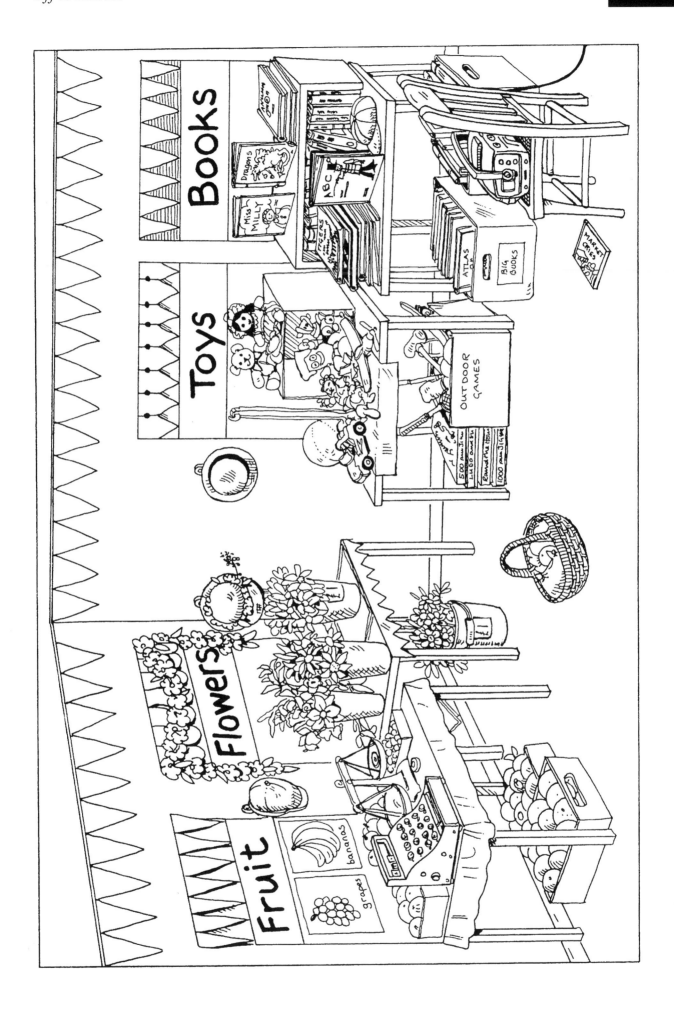

Activity 1   What is for sale at the market?

Teacher's intentions

- To set the scene.
- To encourage reading through repetition.

Speaking together and reading: what's at our market?

Discuss what is sold at the market. Make a list on a large sheet of paper or on a board.

Ask what the customer and market trader might say to each other.

With teacher acting as scribe, write a very simple duologue from their ideas, using one large sheet of paper for each of the characters. For example:

Customer	Market trader
Hello.	*Hello.*
Have you got any bananas?	*Yes. One pound, please.*
Thank you.	*Thank you.*
Goodbye.	*Goodbye.*

Obviously the complexity of the duologue will depend on the age and ability of the children. Read through the duologue with the children pointing to the words. Invite them to join in with you as you continue to point to the words.

Arrange the children in two lines or groups with a duologue script in front of each group so that each half of the class takes the role of either the customer or the market trader. This could be done with small groups taking turns. They conduct the conversation together a few times, with help where necessary.

You might then invite the customer group to choose something else to buy, so they change *banana* for another item. The market trader group can similarly decide how much they will charge for the new item. Nothing else needs to change. The new words could be written on paper and placed over the original words or just changed orally.

The customer may then buy a cake for a hundred pounds!

Maths

Children can write numbers on round pieces of card to make coins, using the various denominations of our coinage. The card may be cut to different sizes to indicate real coins. Children colour them in brown or white/silver according to the currency. They can then try to pay for imagined items or those made in the modelling activity.

Nursery rhymes and songs

Say or sing rhymes and songs that involve markets. See how many you can think of.
Examples include:

To market to market to buy a fat pig
Home again, home again, jiggety jig.
To market, to market to buy a fat hog
Home again, home again, joggety jog.

This little pig went to market
This little pig stayed at home
This little pig had roast beef
This little pig had none
This little pig cried 'Wee-wee-wee'
All the way home.

Sign-making

Create signs showing items for sale at your market stall. These could be pictures only or pictures with words.

Dramatic play: market-day is busy

Those who have been the market traders set up their imaginary stalls in the space and the customers move around buying items from the stalls. The children often use the lines from the duologue with which they are now confident. Others will create their own new dialogue. After a while they can swap roles.

Bring them together and share shopping experiences:

- *What did you buy?*
- *Did they sell nice things?*
- *What was your favourite buy today?*
- *Did you like being the customer or the market trader best?*
- *What did your stall sell? Did you make much money today?*

Visit
Visit a market.

Activity 2 Sounds of the market

Teacher's intentions

- To encourage children to use their voices and fill the space with sounds.
- To practise controlling volume.
- To develop quick responses to signs.

Discussion and calling: the calls of the market

Ask the children if they have heard the calls the market traders use to attract custom to their stall. Provide some examples: 'Two cucumbers for a pound!' 'Cabbage just 50 pence!' Some almost sing out their calls: 'Come and get your carrots here!'

The children can make some up.

The children make groups in the space and imagine they are at their stalls. Invite each group to choose a market call. Let them practise making their calls.

Explain that you will conduct them all together with a baton, but a long paintbrush will do! When your baton is high in the air, they need to be very loud and when your baton is low, they must call quietly.

Then explain that you are someone who has come to the market. As you get nearer to a stall, the call should be louder. As you move away it should get quieter, and then silent again until you return to the vicinity of their stall again. In this way, sometimes there will be a few groups calling at a time and it will be very loud, while at other times you will be able to hear just one call. As you walk into the space, the children concentrate to see if you move near them and when you move away, changing their volume. This creates a collage of market calls.

List of market types
Discuss the different types of market that children have visited, heard about or seen on television: cattle markets, flower markets, antique markets, supermarkets, hypermarkets and so on.

Modelling
Make clay, Plasticine or papier mâché fruit and vegetables to add to the imaginative play area or just for a market stall display.

Vegetable printing

Prepare vegetable cuts for the children to use to print designs on large sheets of paper. Potatoes are good, but many other vegetables work as well and create different textures.

Activity 3   A stranger in the market

Teacher's intentions

- To begin the narrative.
- To encourage children to use their imaginations.

Narration and discussion: who is the stranger?

Narrate:

One day when the market was busy and the air was full of the market traders' calls, a stranger entered the market. No one had ever seen such an amazing sight. A figure in the brightest colours anyone could imagine. He pulled a colourful wagon behind him that seemed to have bells around the wheels. The cart sang beautifully as the wheels turned. Everyone thought the stranger may be singing, too, but he was still too far away for them to work out what he sang.

Discuss what they have heard:

- *What was he like?*
- *What colours might he be wearing?*
- *What do you imagine his clothes to be like?*
- *Describe how you imagine the wagon.*
- *What might be in it?*
- *What could he be singing about?*

The narration continues:

As the jolly figure drew closer, he smiled at everyone and asked if he could sit down in the market square. The people were pleased to have such an exciting excuse to stop their shopping and selling. They sat down, keen to know more about this colourful and happy man. Slowly they began to speak to him and ask him about what was in his wagon, where he had come from and where he was going.

Hot seating with teacher in role: talking to the stranger

The children agree where the teacher in role as the stranger should sit and seat themselves around the spot. Check that they know what they will say to him. The happy stranger enters with a colourful bag and coat (optional). The children ask him questions. He gradually lets them know the following:

Observation drawing

Items from a market stall are arranged for the children to draw.

I am from rainbow land . . . I have travelled to many places for many months. I have a market stall packed up in my wagon . . . I have set up my stall in many places, but have sold nothing. My stall sells only magic items. No one has ever bought anything because they don't believe that my goods are really magic. I say they have to trust me but they don't.

It should be clear that the stranger doesn't 'test' any goods. Their magic will only take effect the following day and he must be trusted.

Would you like me to set up my stall here? Would you buy my things?

Discussion and narration: the stranger's stall

The children discuss what they have heard and decide whether they will believe the strange fellow and his magic. In our experience, children want to believe it and ask him for the market stall, but the discussion about what to decide is important.

The man opened up the back of his wagon as everyone tried to peep inside. He set up a stall and then began to fill it. But the objects weren't bright or colourful like him; they were actually pretty dull-looking: an old kettle, a grubby stone, a pot, a bag of beans and many other strange items. When the stall was so full that it nearly toppled over, the stranger asked each person what they wanted to buy.

In role as the stranger, teacher steps in front of an imaginary stall and looks at it proudly. Then he asks children what they would like to buy. Point excitedly at some of the objects with odd cryptic comments, such as *'You won't be disappointed'*, or *'Oh, yes, the pot'*. He doesn't seem willing or able to say what the magic is or what each item will do. The children must trust him and they will find out for themselves tomorrow. Mime giving any object requested and the exchange of some money.

When everybody in the market square had got what they wanted, the colourful stranger packed up his wagon and left them, a hum on his lips and his wagon wheels jingling. The people all agreed to meet the following day to see if anything had happened.

The stranger, by Charlie

Sound effects

Create the sounds of the market. These will include the calls of the market traders, jingling of money, snippets of conversation, dogs barking, children crying and so on. These are then recorded and used to create atmosphere during the drama.

Activity 4   Stories of magic

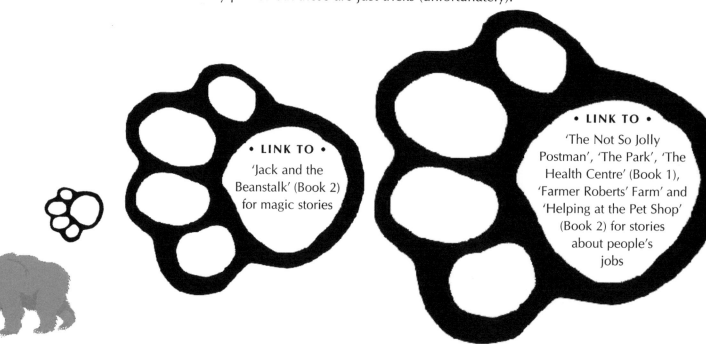

Magic words

Identify and list words we associate with magic such as 'abracadabra'. Make up magic chants.

Teacher's intentions

- To sequence events appropriately.
- To use the children's imaginations.
- To close the story.
- To reflect on the events at the market square.
- To think about the difference between fact and fiction.

Meeting: the magic is real!

Everybody gathered together the following day. Many could not stop smiling because they were so amazed by the magic of their objects. They all wanted to tell their tales and hear about what had happened to the others.

They gather and make up stories about what their objects have done. Perhaps the beans will have made a beanstalk. They can say what they like. Anything goes at this stage! Perhaps a few found that nothing happened. Perhaps it will happen after another day, or maybe it was because they didn't really believe as the stranger said they must.

Discussion: plenary

- What do you think of the stranger?
- Which magic stories did you like?

What might the people do with the magic that has happened (e.g. Will they climb that beanstalk? What might be up here?)?

It is important to make the point that this is only a story and that in real life we should not expect things to be magic! We do see people doing magic at birthday parties but these are just tricks (unfortunately).

• LINK TO •
'Jack and the Beanstalk' (Book 2) for magic stories

• LINK TO •
'The Not So Jolly Postman', 'The Park', 'The Health Centre' (Book 1), 'Farmer Roberts' Farm' and 'Helping at the Pet Shop' (Book 2) for stories about people's jobs

CHAPTER 3

Castle Tales

Queen Juliet wants to build a new castle. She is tired of her old, cold, crumbling castle, which is not big enough for her. She especially wants to build somewhere comfortable for her pet dragon Griffiths to live, sleep and play. Dragons are very rare and she is worried that someone might try to kidnap him. The Queen hires the services of the best craftspeople in the land to design and build the castle, which must be the biggest and best, and be sited in the prime position. When the castle is built a big celebration takes place. All the people who have helped to build the castle are invited to the party. The Queen does not enjoy herself at all as she has heard some terrible news. The ruler of a neighbouring land has kidnapped her pet dragon. Can the Queen's friends help her to rescue the dragon?

Aims

- To practise using appropriate language registers.
- To be able to ask relevant questions to gain specific information.
- To share and develop knowledge about castles.

Themes

- Moral issues: right and wrong.
- Social relationships.
- Castles.

Resources

Optional: Crown or cloak for the two Queens.

- Large sheets of paper and pens.
- Letter (see page 26).

The imaginative play area can be designed as a castle.

Notes

The castle imaginative play area may also be used for many encounters with different teacher roles from various fairy-tales (e.g. Sleeping Beauty, Cinderella, Rumpelstiltskin, Snow White).

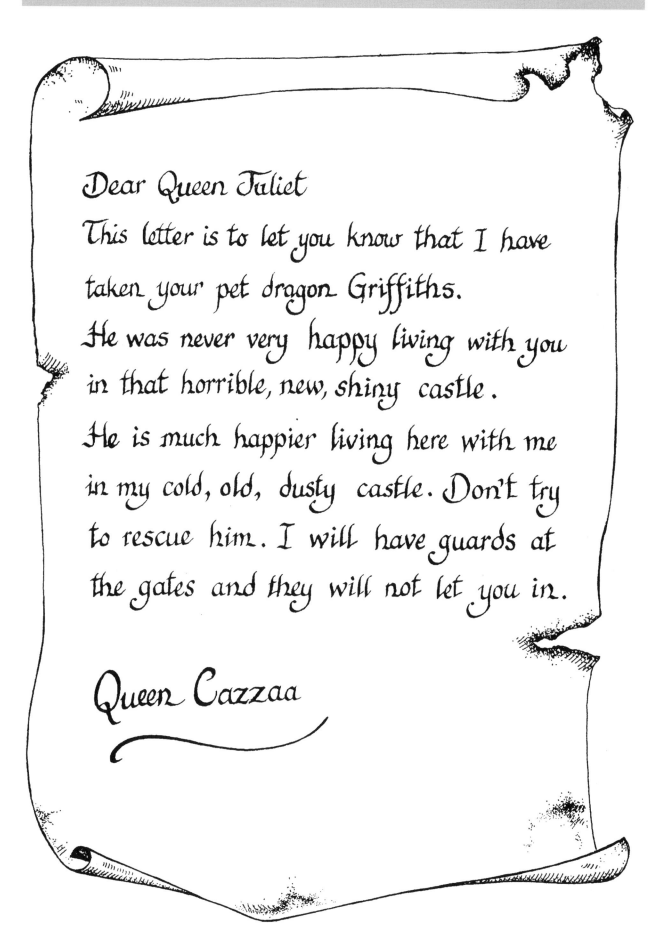

Dear Queen Juliet

This letter is to let you know that I have taken your pet dragon Griffiths.

He was never very happy living with you in that horrible, new, shiny castle.

He is much happier living here with me in my cold, old, dusty castle. Don't try to rescue him. I will have guards at the gates and they will not let you in.

Queen Cazzaa

Activity 1   I need to build a new castle

Teacher's intentions

- To introduce the teacher in role as the Queen.
- To introduce the problem.
- To encourage children to share knowledge of castles.

Teacher in role: the Queen needs help

Tell the children that they are going to listen to the beginning of a story about a Queen, and they will need to find out who they are going to be in the story and what the Queen's problem is.

Welcome everyone. It is so good to have you here today. I know you have travelled from far and wide to answer my plea. I sent all of you letters inviting you to come because I need your help. You are all very experienced people who know everything about building castles, and that is what I need. Some of you are builders who know about stone, some of you are carpenters who know about wood, and some of you are very good at digging. You see, I want to build a new castle to live in. This one is so old and crumbling. It is draughty and the windows don't fit properly. I'm tired of living here. I also need to make sure there is a special room for my pet dragon Griffiths. He is very precious to me and I am afraid someone may try to steal him. But I don't know where to start. I need you to advise me on what I need to think about.

Encourage the children to use their knowledge of castles and to make suggestions. The Queen can make silly suggestions about where to build and what to build the castle out of (e.g. *I'd like it built of wood down in the valley, that would be a good idea, wouldn't it? Oh, it needs to be on the top of a hill, does it? I see. Do you think we could make a list of the things I need to remember? I need big, thick stone walls to keep out attackers, do I?*).

Collective drawing: the Queen's new castle

Use a large sheet of paper and felt-tip pens. Children come up one at a time and draw parts of the castle, using the suggested list of features as a prompt.

Collect...
Pictures of castles, knights, dragons.

Identify castle features
Use a large picture or model of a castle to identify features such as the moat, drawbridge and keep.

Discussion
What do we know about castles?
Who has visited a castle?
Where were castles built?
Why are some castles in ruins?
Who lived in castles?
Who worked there?
Who are knights and what did they do?

Find out...

About the clothing worn by knights and ladies. Why did the knights need armour?

Make...

Shields, swords, bows and arrows and armour from cardboard.

Design...

Your own castle.

Activity 2   Building the castle

Teacher's intentions

- To use mime.
- To build belief in the castle.

Narration and mime: the castle is ready to be built

Encourage the children to join in miming as you narrate the building of the castle. (This can become dramatic play with the children engaged in building the castle on their own without too much direction from the teacher.)

The Queen and the builders had planned a wonderful castle. They collected together all the tools and the equipment that they would need to build the castle. What would they need to do first? We need to measure out where the walls will be.

Arrange the children standing in a square to represent the walls. (Don't forget a space for the door!)

Then encourage the children to mime the building process:

That's a good size. Now we will need to start building the walls with stone. That's it; roll some big stones into place. Don't forget to use lots of mortar to make the stones stick together. Excellent walls. I think we'd better start digging out the moat. Have you got your spades? This is hard work. What about the drawbridge? It's looking wonderful. I'm so pleased with my new castle. What do you think? Now, where are we going to have that special room for Griffiths?

Activity 3   A party to celebrate

Teacher's intentions

- To use descriptive language.
- To introduce tension through the letter from Queen Cazzaa.
- To discuss and make collective decisions.

Whole group improvisation: looking around the new castle

Tell the children that a little while later the builders are all invited to the castle for a tea-party to celebrate the opening of the Queen's new castle. Show the children around the castle, pointing out features and asking them to describe what they see:

You have all worked so hard. I want to show around the castle so you can see how I have decorated it. Let's look in the main hall: what can you see here? Do you like the colour of the throne? Would you like some more tea? Shall we look in the kitchen? Let's go and visit Griffiths in his lovely new room, shall we? Oh no, the door is open. Griffiths isn't here! Where has he gone? What do you think could have happened to him?

Discovery of the letter and discussion: Griffiths is missing

The letter (see page 26) should be 'discovered' rolled up as a scroll and partially hidden.

Wait a minute. There is a piece of paper here. It looks like a letter. I wonder if anyone could help me to read it? I'm in such a dither I can't read properly.

Queen Juliet is helped to read out the letter telling her that Griffiths has been kidnapped. What can be done? Children make suggestions and the group decides which ideas are worth pursuing. These may be improvised if they are feasible, but Queen Juliet usually finds something wrong with each idea (e.g. ringing Queen Cazzaa to speak to her – she will not come to the phone; writing her a letter – this will take too long; making plans to attack her castle – Griffiths might get injured in the fight).

I think it would be a good idea to talk to her face to face about this. Shall I invite her to come here for tea? What do you think? Or should we try to get into her castle by sneaking past the guards? Are you able to creep silently? We'd better have a practice.

Brainstorm...
Words to describe dragons – both friendly and unfriendly.

Game: Grandmother's Footsteps

This game may be used to test the stealth of the children.

One child faces a wall and pretends to be the guard at the palace gate. The others stand in a line next to each other behind her. Their aim is to creep up to her without ever moving when she looks around. If they reach the guard before anyone else, they tap her on the shoulder and win the game. The guard's aim is to make sure that no one achieves this. She must face the wall for a few seconds, then turn around at frequent intervals to try to catch people moving. She can vary the time facing the wall so as to turn around unexpectedly and catch as many children moving as possible. The others attempt to move only when she is facing the wall. If the guard sees them moving or wobbling, she calls their name and they have to go back to where they started. She may send a few back at one go if they are all moving. The game is over when someone touches the guard's shoulder.

Draw...
Individual pictures of dragons. Give them names. Describe them.

That's excellent. You'll have no trouble sneaking past the guards.

Would you talk to her for me? I think I may get too angry. If we get angry she'll never listen to us, will she? We must stay calm and try to talk to her reasonably and persuade her that she is being unfair. What will you say to her?

Narration: getting into Cazzaa's castle

Ask for volunteers to be the guards at the castle. Narrate the approach and successful entry to the castle.

They sneaked quietly up the hill and hid behind a bush until the guards fell asleep. Then silently they began to creep towards the huge castle door…

Read/tell stories

Read/tell stories where castles feature (e.g. Beauty and the Beast).

Music

Use instruments to make up music to accompany a battle or perhaps even spooky music to represent all the phantoms and ghosts that may haunt the castle.

Activity 4   Challenging Queen Cazzaa

Teacher's intentions

● To use persuasion.
● To introduce a teacher role which is in opposition to the group.
● To work together to solve the problem.

Meeting with teacher in role: can we have Griffiths back?

Teacher takes on the role of the naughty Queen Cazzaa. She is surprised that the children have managed to sneak past the guards but is secretly pleased to see them because she doesn't have many visitors.

Children talk to her to try to get her to change her mind about keeping Griffiths. Her arguments for keeping the dragon are:

● She has never had a pet dragon and has always wanted one.
● She is jealous of Queen Juliet's new castle.
● She doesn't see why she shouldn't just take the dragon if she wants it.
● She has always had everything she wanted.
● She has no one to talk to and play with.

The children need to find ways of persuading her that she is doing wrong. They may perhaps suggest she gets a pet of her own.

Discussion: plenary

● Which characters did the children meet in the castle adventure?
● What help did they have to give to Queen Juliet?
● Why was Queen Cazzaa so nasty?
● How did they manage to persuade her to return Griffiths to Queen Juliet?

• LINK TO •
'The Jungle' and 'Helping at the Pet Shop' (Book 2) and 'The Lonely Dragon' (Book 3) for animals

• LINK TO •
'The Lost Hat' and 'Goldilocks' (Book 1), 'Jack and the Beanstalk' (Book 2) and 'Finders Keepers' (Book 3) for stealing

CHAPTER 4

Forest Adventure

A woodcutter who lives in the forest has not had much luck in his life. He lives alone in a house that needs everything repaired. He can't put things right on his own. One day, when he ventures deep into the forest to collect firewood, he loses his way. Dark and cold, he huddles under a tree. A spirit, the magic Mushkil Gusha, appears before him offering food and a fine fur to keep him warm. Mushkil Gusha explains that if he always gives food to someone who is hungry on a Friday his luck will change. The woodcutter is grateful and, the following Friday, although he has little himself, he shares his food with a beggar.

Things strangely begin to change. The house is transformed and all should be well, but in time the woodcutter forgets the request of Mushkil Gusha. His luck fades away. The neighbours must persuade the very reluctant woodcutter to share his food again on Fridays.

The children are creatively involved in making the forest and the house and representing its change in fortune.

This drama is based very loosely on an ancient Iranian tale called 'The Magic of Mushkil Gusha' in *Persian Tales*, collected and translated by D.L.R. and E.O. Lorimer, published by Macmillan in 1919.

Aims

- To encourage thought for others.
- To consider responsibility for promises made.
- To develop the imagination.
- For children to work creatively with their bodies.

Themes

- Forests.
- Promises.
- Social responsibility.

Resources

Optional: www.aaronshep.com/Stories/048.html. This website provides a lovely retelling of the tale set in its original context beside a desert. Where this story is told on the site there is also background information about the story, such as why Friday was significant.

The imaginative play area can be designed as a forest or a neglected house.

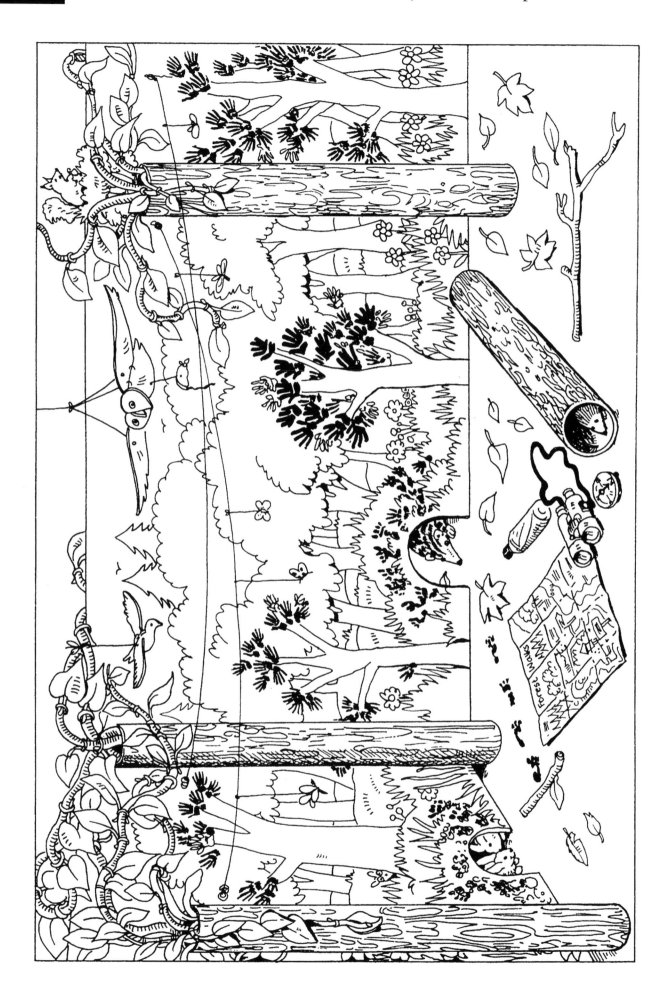

Activity 1   A house by the forest

Teacher's intentions

- To set the scene.
- To construct the house creatively.
- To practise physical control.

Narration and dramatic construction: the woodcutter's life

Narrate:

At the edge of a forest lives a woodcutter. He has not had a lot of luck in his life. He loves living by the forest and spends most days collecting wood that he can sell to his friends and neighbours. He doesn't really make enough money to buy clothes and food. His house is in a terrible mess. Once it was a fine house with a proud front gate and solid fence, and a beautiful garden with fruit trees. But now everything from the chimney-pots to the walls needs mending. It doesn't even keep the rain out!

The children discuss what the house would have looked like when it was beautiful, considering its size, shape, windows and garden. Then, one by one, the children should stand in a position to represent a part of the house. You could ask for the front door first. A child stands as the door and could describe it briefly. A couple of children could then be asked to make the gate, considering where they should stand in relation to the door. The fence is added, the fruit trees, the walls of the house and the windows. Two tall children could reach up their arms to be the chimney-pots. Each child should be part of the beautiful house.

As they stand, explain that now the house has tumbled down and everything needs to be repaired. Count to three, and on three, the children must turn the house into what it has become. The door may bend over to signify that it doesn't fit the door frame, and a tree's branches may now hang low. You could count to three again and ask the house to be as it was and then back again to what it has become. The children will enjoy the changes. You could ask some children to describe what has happened to them. Ask the children to add sound effects such as creaks, groans, cracks and sighs.

Other Iranian stories

Look up other stories from Iranian sources. Some may be classified as from 'Persia' which was the name given previously to Iran: www.aaronshep.com/indexes/genre.html.

Read the story of 'The Magic of Mushkil Gusha'

The retelling of the story is on www.aaronshep.com/Stories/048.html.

Rhyme

Learn the rhyme:
There was a crooked man
who walked a crooked mile.
He had a crooked sixpence and
he climbed a crooked style.
He had a crooked cat that caught
a crooked mouse
And they all lived together in
a crooked little house.

Geography

Find Iran on a map or globe.

Tree study

Collect leaves from different types of tree. Children match their leaves with pictures of different tree and leaf types, and learn the names of the trees.

Activity 2   Lost in the forest

Teacher's intentions

- To take the story further.
- To introduce the children to the magic.

Narration and teacher in role: creating the forest

Narrate:

One day, the woodcutter goes deep into the forest to collect firewood, but as it gets darker he loses his way. The wind is whistling more strongly than usual through the trees, which look dark and tall. He is sure they are whispering to him that he is lost and will never find his way home. He can't recognise the paths at all. At last, tired, cold, hungry and afraid, he huddles at the foot of a tree.

Invite discussion to clarify understanding of what has been told:

- *Where is the woodcutter?*
- *What is he doing there?*
- *Why isn't he at home?*
- *What might he think the trees are whispering to him?*

Ask the children to spread about in the space as the trees. They can make the sounds of the wind or maybe owls. Teacher will be in role as the woodcutter wandering frightened among them. When he passes a child, the child can whisper at him, using the ideas discussed (e.g. *'You are lost.' 'You will never get home.'*). The woodcutter finally huddles at the foot of one of the children and looks about him, terrified.

Forest walk

Talk about smells, colours and textures. Collect stones, leaves and twigs to take back for a display table. The items could be named.

Then ask the children to sit down in a group and narrate:

The following day some neighbours were out walking in the forest and found the woodcutter fast asleep under the tree with a thick, expensive fur blanket over him and a hamper of unfinished food beside him. They couldn't understand what could have happened. They woke him to ask what was happening.

The teacher sits down in role as the woodcutter and answers their questions, giving the following information:

A figure I knew to be the powerful and magic Mushkil Gusha appeared before me in the forest last night. I had heard of this magician in stories my grandmother told me. I could hardly believe it myself. The proof is over me and beside me! How could I now have such a fine fur or such a luxurious hamper without magic?

Mushkil Gusha said that I must always share my food with someone who is hungry on Fridays before dark and my luck will change. I thanked him for the fur and the food and promised I would.

Please, share this good food. It is Friday today!

Tree bark rubbings

Make bark rubbings with paper and wax crayons against different trees. Match them up and name the different trees.

You may be asked what the figure was wearing or how you knew it was Mushkil Gusha. Make up any additional pieces of information. Most children will not have heard of this figure, but it won't matter if you say you have heard stories about him and his magic.

Activity 3   Promises remembered and promises forgotten

Teacher's intentions

- To construct an activity which demands very close listening skills.
- To reuse the image of the house to represent the woodcutter's fortunes.

Narration and action: promises remembered

Narrate:

Every Friday, the woodcutter shared his food, however little there was, with someone who was hungry. His luck started to change. Strange things happened. A young man passed by who wanted to learn about house building and offered to help the woodcutter repair his house. The two of them changed the house back to how it used to be.

Recreate the house as it was when it was neglected, and narrate the changes to bring them about from the children (e.g. *They repaired the door so that it fitted the door frame. They mended the fence so it was strong enough to withstand the strong winds*). The house gradually changes back to the beautiful house that they had first constructed in Activity 1.

> **Images of Mushkil Gusha**
>
> Discuss what the magic spirit may have looked like. What size, colour, shape was he? Draw pictures of him.

Narration and action: promises forgotten

Narration continues while the children are still representing the house. They again respond to the narration:

As time passed, however, the woodcutter began to forget about sharing on Fridays, and sometimes he felt he wanted all his food to himself. Gradually, good luck stopped coming his way. In fact, some unlucky things began to happen. A huge tree fell on to one side of his house, knocking down part of the fence, the gate and part of the house.

Indicate which children need to react and fall to the ground.

One night, a very strong wind blew out many windows and knocked the chimney-pots down. There was no passerby keen to rebuild the house. Strangely, his trees no longer bore fine, juicy fruit, and it seemed harder than ever to find enough firewood in the forest. The woodcutter sat wondering what had all gone wrong.

> **Magic figure connections with other stories**
>
> Consider other figures with magical powers in familiar fairy stories (e.g. the fairy godmother in Cinderella and the old woman who gives Jack the magic beans that grow into a beanstalk). Think about magical characters who give magic and want something in return (e.g. Rumpelstiltskin (a wife) and the Pied Piper of Hamelin (money)). Mushkil Gusha wants the woodcutter to share his food with the hungry. Are there any other figures like this in fairy stories?

Activity 4   Can the neighbours help?

Teacher's intentions

- To encourage the articulation of ideas.
- To reflect upon the story.
- To relate the story to our own lives.

Hot seating and teacher in role: talking to the woodcutter

Sit the children down in a group again. Ask them why they think the wood-cutter's luck has changed. How could he have forgotten about Mushkil Gusha and his promises? They are invited, in role as the neighbours, to speak to him.

Teacher in role as the woodcutter is not easy to talk to:

- *You don't believe that stuff, do you?*
- *That was just a dream I had in the forest that night.*
- *I hadn't got enough food to keep sharing it anyway.*
- *If I share anything again, I will be even poorer. That would be crazy.*
- *I'm the one who needs people to share their food with me now!*

They will probably put up a big enough argument to make the woodcutter try sharing his food again. They can then agree how the story will end. They may like to rebuild the house and one of them could narrate the end of the story as they have agreed it.

Discussion: plenary

If Mushkil Gusha came to us, what might he ask us to do every week? We may not know people who have no food, so what sorts of things might we be able to do:

- At home?
- At school?

• LINK TO •
'Jack and the Beanstalk' (Book 2) and 'Off to Market' (Book 3) for magical power

• LINK TO •
'Goldilocks' (Book 1), 'Jack and the Beanstalk' and 'Cinderella' (Book 2) and 'Billy Goats Gruff' and 'Humpty Dumpty' (Book 3) for traditional stories

5 The Red Garden

Crimson Rouge loves the colour red. Everything in her house is red: red carpets, red curtains, and she even has a red parrot. Now she would like to turn her attention to her garden. Crimson is a very enthusiastic gardener but doesn't quite know what she's doing. She lacks the knowledge and skills to put her ideas into practice. That is, until she advertises for some help in the garden and her new friends teach her about the different tools she needs and the plants she can grow. One day, Crimson hears about a very special red flower growing in a forest in the mountains. She asks her friends to go on an expedition with her to find a specimen of the plant for her garden. When they arrive, things are not quite so straightforward. This is the last specimen of its kind left in the world. Will Crimson be persuaded to leave the plant or is she just too selfish?

Aims

- To share knowledge and understanding of growing plants.
- To be aware that there are rare species of plants and animals that must be protected.
- To discuss people's obsessions.

Themes

- Gardens.
- Growing.
- Conservation.
- Rare species.
- Moral issues: right and wrong.

Resources

A plan of Crimson's garden.
Optional: Red clothes for Crimson to wear.

The imaginative play area can be designed as a garden or a garden shed.

Notes

Crimson has been written as a woman but there is no reason why the role should not be male. If you prefer to focus on an alternative colour to red, please feel free!

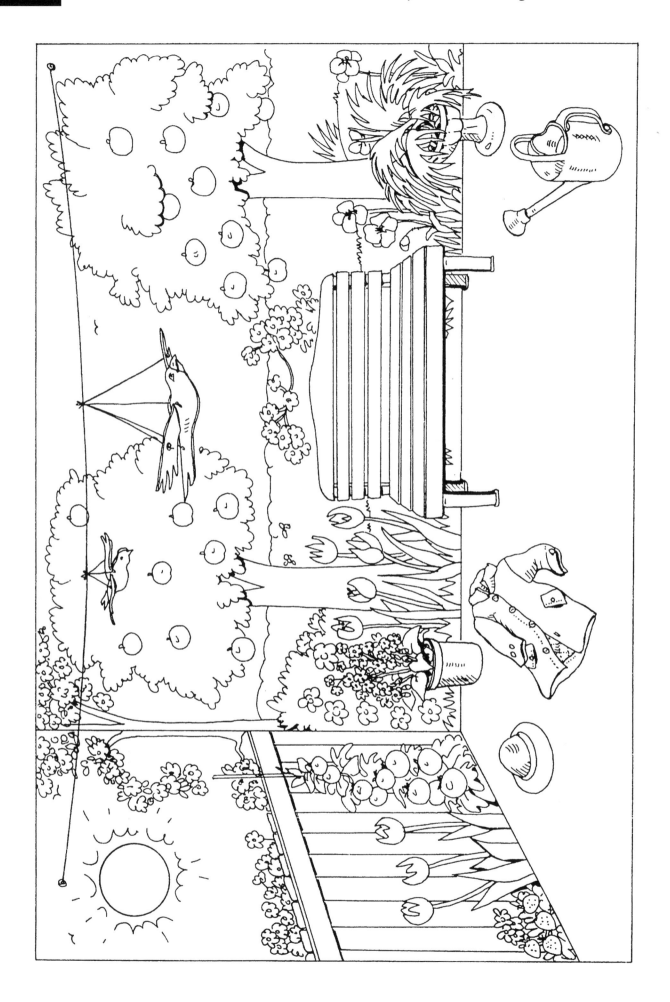

Activity 1   Meeting Crimson Rouge

Teacher's intentions

- To introduce the teacher role.
- To set the scene.
- To invest in individual roles.

Monologue: setting the scene

Explain to the children that you are going to tell them about yourself in role as the character in the drama. They should listen and pick up information. There will be a chance to ask questions later.

Good morning everyone. It's so good to see you all. When I advertised for people to help me in my garden I never expected so many replies. There's plenty to do, so don't worry! Now, I must introduce myself. My name is Crimson Rouge and as you can see I love the colour red. I love red so much that everything in my house is red. Now I really want a red garden but I'm not very good at gardening. That's why you're here. I need ideas. Have you got any questions you'd like to ask me?

What do we know so far? Who are the children in the drama? Who are you? Is there anything the children need to find out? Clarify that everyone understands what is happening before going on to the next activity.

Hot seating: what do we need to know about Crimson?

Tell the children that they can ask the teacher questions in role. Replies are given with the following information in mind:

- Crimson wants a beautiful garden with only red flowers. She realises that she can't have red grass but she wants red water in the pond and red rocks.
- She's not sure whether there are red trees or not.
- She could have a plan of the garden to show the children.

Thank you everyone. I hope you are all clear about what I'm looking for. Would you like to look around the garden now?

Discussion

Does everyone have a garden?
What do we do in the garden?
What kinds of things might we find in a garden?

Stories and poems

Stories, poems and rhymes about gardens. *This Little Puffin* by Elizabeth Matterson has a chapter of rhymes ('In the garden').

Literacy

Crimson Rouge is an unusual name. Think of other names that could be related to colours. Try starting with other words for red such as cherry, ruby, burgundy. Put them into pairs and see if they sound like names. Try other colours such as:

- Green (emerald, olive, lime).
- Blue (azure, cobalt, navy, sapphire, indigo).
- Yellow (golden, blond).
- Purple (violet, mauve, lilac, lavender, plum, amethyst).

Children can choose a name for themselves to use in the drama.

Collective drawing

The children can be asked to draw tools and equipment on to an outline of a garden shed.

Activity 2   Working in the garden

Teacher's intentions

- To engage in improvisation.
- To share knowledge of gardening and tools.

Improvisation: looking around the garden

Crimson leads the gardeners around the garden showing them the grass, the pond, the greenhouse and the shed. She opens the door of the shed.

There are lots of tools in here but I don't know what they are for. Could you help me?

[Picking up an imaginary spade.] *This is a spade, I think.* [Accentuate the pronounciation of the word so that it sounds strange: s – p – a – de. Try to make out that she is unfamiliar with the vocabulary – spade, rake, hoe – so they will have to correct her.] *What do you do with it? Could you show me how to use it? Oh, you put this end in the ground, do you? It's hard work. What about this? I think it's a rake. Could you show me? What do I need this watering can for? There's a machine here for cutting the grass but I don't know how it works.*

The garden helpers show Crimson what to do with all of the tools.

Dramatic play with teacher in role: working in the garden

Thank you for showing me how to use the tools. Now I'll be able to help you, won't I? Shall we get started?

Encourage the helpers to decide which tool they want to use and start work. Crimson goes around asking questions and making rather silly comments which the children can easily put right, for example:

I can use this trowel to cut the grass, can't I? These shears are for digging, aren't they? If I plant an acorn it will grow into a rose-bush, won't it?

In the garden, by Charlie

Activity 3   Crimson has a plan

Teacher's intentions

- To introduce a problem.
- To move the drama on.

Discussion in role: I have some interesting news

In role as Crimson, call all the helpers together and tell them you have some exciting news. You have just read an article in the newspaper about a very rare red flower called the 'Carmine Vermilion' that has been found growing deep in a forest on the island of Telracs. You want them to go and bring one home for your garden. Say that you hope all your helpers will be willing to go on the trip to the mountain with you and that they will be well paid. You won't be going, as you need to stay at home to look after the new garden. Tell them that they must bring the plant home at all costs. Ask them to suggest what equipment they will need to take on a trip to the mountains. Write a list of things needed or draw items into a pre-drawn outline of a suitcase or backpack (see circle activity).

Narration with mimed action: going to the island of Telracs

Tell the children that they are getting ready for the journey, and narrate:

Everyone began to pack their bags to go on the trip. They first packed their clothes, then their toothbrushes, then their shoes. Some packed a teddy or a photo of their family.

Continue in the same style using the ideas as discussed by the children in the previous activity or in the circle activity.

Narrate the journey including the plane ride, walking through the forest, seeing various animals, crossing a stream and so on. This section can be as short or as long as you like, depending on the involvement of the children. You can also stop the narration at any point and ask the children to freeze. They can then be thought tapped to find out how they are feeling about any aspect of the journey.

Activity 4   Finding the Carmine Vermilion

Teacher's intentions

- To use persuasive language.
- To encourage children to put forward a point of view.
- To encourage skills for making a case.
- To discuss wider issues of the destruction of the natural environment and the need to protect rare species.

Visit…
A local garden centre or look around the school grounds or wildlife garden.

Drawing
Draw an outline of a suitcase or a backpack. Ask the children to come forward one at a time and draw an item of equipment they would need to take on an expedition to the jungle (e.g. rope, binoculars, water-bottle).

Shared writing
Make a seed catalogue. Think of new names for the flowers and describe them in the catalogue.

Matching

Identify and then match names to pictures of well-known flowers (e.g. daffodil, daisy, tulip, rose).

Narration: what a beautiful plant

Eventually after searching all night and all day they saw something glowing red between the trees. This must be it. They crept closer and saw the most beautiful flower they had ever seen. They stood around the flower and gazed at it.

Ask the children to describe the flower, the scent and the leaves.

As they all stood there looking in amazement, out stepped an old woman from behind a tree.

Discussion in role: 'You can't take that plant!'

You have had a long journey, I see. You look very tired. Would you like to sit down here in the clearing? How did you hear about this flower? What do you think about it now that you have seen it? Have you come to take some photographs or make a sketch?

When the helpers tell her what they have come to do the old woman gets very upset and tells them that this is the last specimen of its kind in the world and if it is moved it may not make any seed. They can't possibly move it. It belongs here in the forest and not in someone's garden. It is for everyone to see. There have been other beautiful flowers that have died out (become extinct) because people have been greedy and not looked after them. The helpers may try to argue their case.

The children will have to decide the outcome of the story. Either way the end can be narrated:

When they returned home without the flower, Crimson was furious and they had to explain why it was better to leave the flower in the forest. She eventually understood and went on the journey herself so that she could see it in all its glory in its natural place.

Or:

When they returned home with the flower, Crimson was so excited and planted it in the garden. But the flower didn't do well and died. There will never be another Carmine Vermilion. One person's greed means that that beautiful flower is now extinct.

Collect

and look at seed catalogues and pictures of different flowers.

Design

Design new flowers and plants or design a garden. This could be done collectively or in groups. Children could brainstorm garden features that should be included and must make sure to incorporate them in their plans.

Plenary discussion

Discuss the issues raised in the story about the greed of individuals, and also about plants and animals becoming extinct.

• LINK TO •
'Under the Sea' (Book 2), 'Finders Keepers' (Book 3) and 'Pirate Adventure' (Book 2) for moral issues

• LINK TO •
'Baz the Vandal' and 'The Dirty River' (Book 1) and 'In the Jungle' (Book 2) for stories about caring for the environment

6 Humpty Dumpty

Everyone enjoys this nursery rhyme, chanting it with claps and moves. But when the children meet Humpty Dumpty they are surprised to find that he sits on the wall because he is fed up. Other children don't want to play with him because he is different. He can't help being an egg. He was born this way. His mother says he should be proud to be an egg, like his parents and grandparents before him. He finds it difficult to be glad to be an egg, however, especially when it means that the children laugh at him and exclude him from their games.

Aims

- To encourage a celebration of difference.
- To develop empathy.
- To practise coordination and a sense of rhythm.

Themes

- Prejudice.
- Considering the feelings of others.
- Nursery rhymes.

Resources

Humpty Dumpty 'rhyme' (see p. 44).

The imaginative play area can be designed as Nursery Rhyme Land.

Humpty Dumpty
sat on a wall.
Humpty Dumpty
had a great fall.
All the king's horses
and all the king's men
Couldn't put Humpty together again!

Humpty Dumpty, by Charlie

Activity 1   Saying the rhyme

Teacher's intentions

- To develop a sense of rhythm.
- To encourage physical coordination.

Speaking together: getting to know the rhyme

Say the rhyme to the children. Then invite them all to join in.

Divide the group into two: half say the first two lines and half say the second two lines about the King's horses and men.

Clapping with the rhyme: playing with the rhythm

1   Clap with every other beat, i.e. on 'Hump' and 'Dump' . . . 'all', 'horses'.

2   Clap on both thighs rather than hands together. Keep to every other beat.

3   Try clapping with hands for the first two lines and then moving to the thighs for lines three and four.

4   With older or particularly well-coordinated children, try moving from handclaps to thigh claps alternatively.

5   This could be developed into a range of different ways of marking the beat (e.g. clap hands on head with every 'Hump' and 'Dump', or stamp feet during the King's horses lines three and four). The children can make suggestions.

Making gestures: playing with the meaning

Discuss what action could be made for the first line. It may be a rounding gesture with both hands to indicate the shape of Humpty Dumpty, or it could focus on him sitting on a wall, or perhaps both. Practise saying the line together with the action.

Do the same for each of the four lines and say them together in a large circle so that the whole rhyme is recited with actions for each line.

Egg drawings

Eggs, either empty or hard boiled, can be decorated for Easter or made into characters like Humpty Dumpty with faces and hair drawn on them.

Nursery rhymes

Discuss and chant other nursery rhymes.

Actions with Humpty Dumpty

The children mime actions to accompany their delivery of the rhyme of Humpty Dumpty. They can be sitting on the wall, fall off, and then be the King's men marching to the scene, only to scratch their heads since they don't know what to do to help Humpty.

Papier mâché egg figures

Cover a blown-up balloon with strips of newspaper dipped in paste. Leave it to dry. The hardened shells can be painted and sculpted further with papier mâché or with fabric. Pipe cleaners could be used for thin arms and legs.

Cooking

Demonstrate how to cook boiled eggs.

Different versions

Look at different versions of Humpty Dumpty. Ask the children if they know any alternative versions, for example:

Humpty Dumpty sat on a wall,
Eating green bananas
Where do you think he put the skin?
Down the King's pyjamas!

There is a selection of alternative versions in *The Puffin Book of Nursery Rhymes* by Iona and Peter Opie. It is interesting to compare the versions and to look for similarities and differences. Children always enjoy listening to and learning the German version.

Activity 2   Talking to Humpty Dumpty

Teacher's intentions

- To listen to someone's thoughts and feelings.
- To develop empathy.
- To consider difference.

Hot seating: why does Humpty sit on the wall?

Ask the children why they think Humpty might have been sitting on the wall which, after all, seems a pretty dangerous place to sit! Discuss any ideas and then explain that they can meet Humpty while he is still on the wall to try to find out. Consider how the conversation might be started.

Teacher in role as Humpty sits on a chair or box to indicate the wall and looks sad and dejected. The children sit in a group in front of Humpty and ask him why he sits there. Humpty may take a while to feel able to speak to the children. This makes the children work hard to find the right voice and questions to reassure Humpty that they are interested. The information should not be given quickly. The children find out that Humpty feels rejected by other children who don't want to play with him because he is different. He can't help being an egg. He was born this way. His mother says he should be proud to be an egg, like his parents and grandparents before him. He finds it difficult to be glad to be an egg, however, especially when it means that the children laugh at him and exclude him from their games.

Examples of Humpty's responses are:

- *You can't really be interested in talking to me.*
- *Why don't you talk to the other children over there?*
- *Everyone loves to talk and play with them.*
- *Are you really interested in talking to me? No one usually is.*
- *I wanted to join in their games, but they won't let me.*
- *They laugh at me. They call me 'scrambled' or 'poached'.*
- *They think it's so funny, but it doesn't feel funny to me.*
- *I know when they laugh* with *people and when they laugh* at *people. Do you know what I mean?*
- *My parents say I should be proud of who I am, but it's not very easy.*
- *My grandma says others should be happy to have friends who aren't all boringly the same. She says she has all sorts of friends.*
- *But Grandma doesn't know the children at my school.*
- *What should I say/do?*

Activity 3   Addressing the problem

Teacher's intentions

- To develop the skills required to argue a moral case.
- To encourage children to stick to what is right despite pressure to do otherwise.

Group meeting: approaching the children

Invite comments about what the children think about Humpty's predicament. What would they like to say to the other children? Tell them that it may be a bit frightening to speak to crowds of children, but you can arrange for them to speak to one of the children so they can explain what they think and what Humpty thinks.

Teacher takes the role of a belligerent child who doesn't seem to care what Humpty thinks. S/he doesn't want to play with a stupid egg anyway! The children have the task of trying to change the child's attitude. You will need to vary your role depending on how forceful the children are. You may hold out for a while and say nasty things about Humpty if they seem strong enough to argue with you. Alternatively, you may need to be prepared to show that you might be wrong earlier in the conversation. You might concede that he plays marbles pretty well, for example, or that you wouldn't like it if no one played with you.

Ideally, the children bring the child around to a more sensitive, unprejudiced position, and they may suggest that s/he goes to speak to Humpty.

Drawings of Humpty Dumpty

Look at the different ways that Humpty Dumpty is presented in books or children's items, such as place mats. Ask the children how they imagine him to look. Is he wearing a hat? Does he look happy or sad? Are we supposed to like him, smile about him or feel sorry for him?
Look at the images on the website:
www.art.com/asp/display-aspp/-/—13061/Humpty_Dumpty_art_htm.
Individual or groups can make drawings of Humpty Dumpty.

Websites

There are many websites with nursery rhymes. Many offer little. However, the following may be of interest:
www.indianchild.com/humpty%20dumpty.htm.
This site offers a musical rendition of the rhyme and many other nursery rhymes.
www.art.com/asp/display-aspp/-/—13061/Humpty_Dumpty_art_htm. You can order posters of different images of Humpty Dumpty from this site. There are some samples on display at the site which may lead to a range of ideas of how Humpty might be presented.
www.Newton.mec.edu/Angier./DimSum/Poetry%20Nursery%20Lesson.html. This site offers a range of traditional Chinese nursery rhymes and lesson suggestions.

Shared writing

The teacher leads shared writing of a unique verse of Humpty Dumpty which the children create. The emphasis is on generating a rhyme. Starter lines could be:

Humpty Dumpty went to bed
Slipped and fell and broke his _____,

Or:

Humpty Dumpty sat in a tree
His mother brought him a cup
of _____.

Letter writing

Write a shared letter to the children to explain to them how Humpty feels. Letters could also be written from Humpty himself, or from the children to Humpty once they understand the issues.

Activity 4   Reflecting on the story

Teacher's intentions

● To consider Humpty's position.

● To consider Humpty's difference positively.

Discussion: understanding Humpty's feelings

● Why did Humpty feel different?

● Why didn't the children want to play with him?

● If there were lots of other eggs in the playground, would it have made it easier for Humpty?

● Would the other children have played with the eggs if there were lots of eggs?

● What could we say to Humpty to make him feel happier?

● What could we say to Humpty to make him feel stronger?

● What might Humpty be able to do well because he is an egg? (E.g. roll down a hill faster than any of the others?)

These are, of course, very difficult questions with no simple answers. The drama and the questions obviously concern wider issues of prejudice that disadvantages children both in and out of school.

Investigation

Investigate eggs. Where do they come from? Look at the shell and describe it – colour, shape, texture. Crack the egg. Look at the yolk and the white. Think about ways in which we cook and eat eggs (e.g. boil, fry, scramble, poach).

Science/knowledge and understanding

Talk about other types of birds' eggs (e.g. duck, quail, swan, emu, ostrich). Make a collection or look at pictures.

• LINK TO •

'Goldilocks' (Book 1), 'Jack and the Beanstalk' and 'Cinderella' (Book 2) and 'Billy Goats Gruff' (Book 3) for traditional stories

• LINK TO •

'Goldilocks' (Book 1), 'Mary Mary and the Giant', 'All for One and One for All' and 'Under the Sea' (Book 2) and 'The Lonely Dragon' and 'Finders Keepers' (Book 3) for moral issues

7 The Toymaker's Workshop

The toymaker makes wonderful toys for children. She is getting so many orders for her toys that she needs to employ more staff to work with her. Tonica the toymaker and her apprentices (the children) design and make new toys, but they also mend old toys that are worn out. They meet Charlie Bear, who was once a much-loved bear but now sits alone on a shelf covered in dust. Charlie Bear's owner now has new toys to play with and he is feeling very neglected. They also receive a visit from a representative for a large toy company (or Father Christmas, if it is an appropriate time of the year), who wants designs for some new traditional toys. Can the apprentices rise to these challenges?

Aims

- To provide problem-solving opportunities.
- To encourage group work.
- To create opportunities for a range of different speaking registers.
- To bring about a consideration of care and responsibilities.

Themes

- Helping others.
- Toys.
- Design.

Resources

Optional

- Costume suggestions: Tonica the toymaker – overall or apron, clipboard and pen; Charlie Bear – brown coat, scarf, gloves; Rupert – briefcase, large letter addressed to the toymaker (see p. 51).
- Large sheet of paper and felt-tip pens.
- Art and DT materials.

The imaginative play area can be designed as the toymaker's workshop.

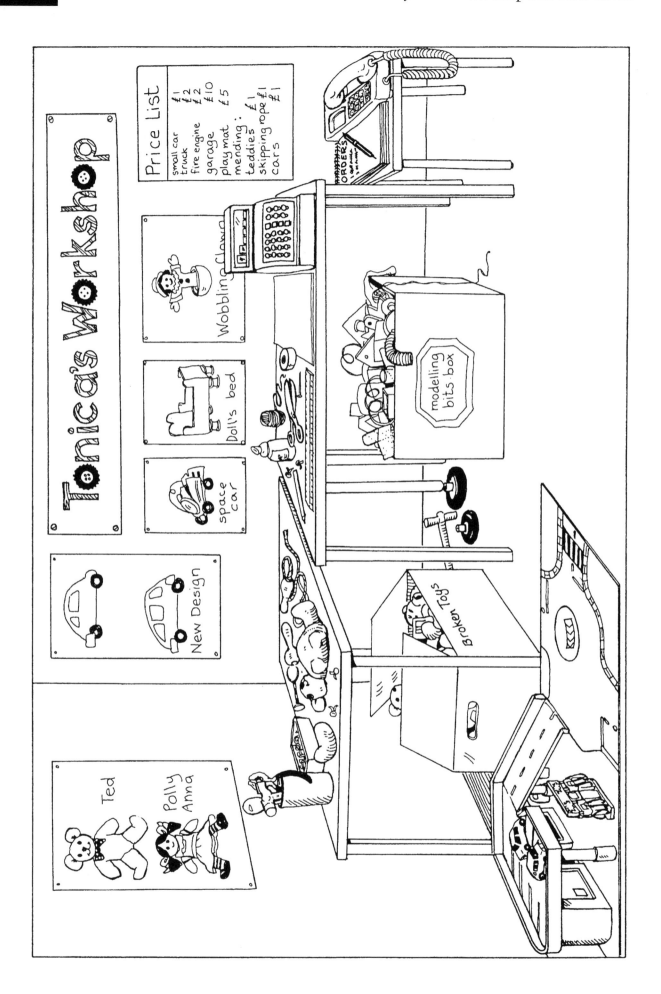

Toby's Toy Shop

Dear Tonica,

We have heard that you are a wonderful toymaker.

We would like you to design and make some new toys that could be sold in our shop. We already have enough electronic toys and ones that use batteries. We really want some old-fashioned toys. Toys that you push and pull would be wonderful. Also, toys that you throw and toys you can cuddle.

Please could you make the toys from:

wood

paper

cardboard

material

Rupert will give you more details.

Best wishes,

Mr Toby (Owner)

Activity 1   Introducing Tonica's toy workshop

Teacher's intentions

- To introduce the context for the drama.
- To develop listening skills.
- To introduce the teacher role of Tonica.

Storytelling: setting the scene

Tell the children that you are going to tell a story about the toyshop today. Will they help?

Once there was a toymaker who loved to make toys for children. She had a workshop where she made all the toys and a small shop where people came to buy them. She made some wonderful toys. She made … and … (children discuss ideas). Her toys were so popular that one day she decided that she needed some help. Lots of people wanted to work in the shop but she chose the best people, the ones who knew lots about toys.

Would you like to be those people who help Tonica the toymaker? I am going to be Tonica the toymaker now. I'll walk in and start to talk to you.

Discussion: what should we make at the workshop?

Hello everyone, it's lovely to see you all here today. I'm very pleased that so many people who know about toys are coming to work with me. My mother taught me everything I know about making toys and I have no children of my own. I'd like to teach you all how to make toys and then you will be able to carry on in the workshop when I'm too old. Will you tell me your names and what kind of toys you know most about? What will you be good at making? Do you know what materials you will need to make that?

At the toyshop, by Charlie

Activity 2   Discovering what's in the workshop

Teacher's intentions

- To practise physical control.
- To develop the context of the workshop.
- To experience the fun of imagining toys coming alive.

Still image: looking around the workshop

Would you like to look around the workshop?

The children create a still picture showing the toys in the workshop. Either ask the children to choose which toy they would like to be in the workshop or the children can all be the same toy at the same time. Tell them that you will count to three, then clap your hands and they will all stand completely still (like statues) to show what toy they are. Walk around the workshop looking at all the toys and commenting about them.

Narration: looking around the workshop

One, two, three, Freeze. Here is the workshop where I make all the toys. Here are the spinning-tops, here are the racing cars and here are the soft toys. These are some of the best-selling toys I make. We have a great demand for these at Christmas. The children love them. Do you know something secret? At night when the lights are out in the shop the toys come to life. Shall we see what they do?

Dramatic play: the workshop comes to life

If possible, turn out the lights in the room. When the lights are out the children can move around the room as the toys. When you turn the lights on again they must return quickly to their places and become completely still, because someone may be coming. No one must know that the toys come to life! When they have returned to their places, they can begin to move about again when the lights go out again and they think the coast is clear. Music from *The Nutcracker Suite* by Tschaikovsky could also be played during this activity. The music being suddenly turned off could replace the turning on and off of lights as the cue for the toys to return to their original places. Alternatively, hand-claps can be the signal to move and stop.

Music and dance…
Tchaikovsky's *The Nutcracker Suite*. The story and music may be found on website: http:www.waltm.net/ nutcrack.htm.

Games (see Book 2, Pirates)
Musical Statues and Grandmother's Footsteps.

Stories

Read stories about toys (e.g. *Old Bear Stories* by Jane Hissey or *Dogger* by Shirley Hughes).

Activity 3   Meeting Charlie Bear

Teacher's intentions

- To encourage empathy.
- To develop an awareness of the effect of different voices.
- To engender a caring attitude.

Teacher in role: introducing Charlie Bear's problem

Before we start making any new toys, we have lots of old ones that have been sent here to be mended. We'd better start on those. Oh yes, I have a bit of a problem that you might be able to help me out with. Charlie Bear was brought in yesterday. He looks very sad and I haven't been able to get him to talk to me. I wonder if you could have a chat with him and find out what's wrong?

Discussion: deciding what to say and how to say it

Ask the children to think of the best way to coax Charlie Bear into talking to them.

How might they tell him that they are sorry that he is sad?

The children suggest questions that could be asked. Practise asking questions. Focus on how the question is asked.

Should we shout at Charlie Bear if he is silent? What kind of voice might make him feel safe with us? Let's practise using a soft voice so we don't frighten him.

Tell the children you are going to be Charlie Bear in the next part of the story.

Maths

Draw a graph to show favourite toys. How many children prefer jigsaws or dolls?

Hot seating: meeting Charlie Bear

The children meet the teacher in role as Charlie Bear. They try to persuade him to talk. He is eventually coaxed to trust them and he gives the following information in response to their questions.

- *I'm a very old bear.*
- *I'm a bit tatty now as I've been hugged and cuddled so much.*
- *My squeaker doesn't work any more.*
- *My ear is torn and my button eye is loose.*
- *My owner has just had a birthday and had loads of new toys so I've now been put on a shelf and am covered in dust.*
- *If you mend me, I may be able to sit on the end of his bed again.*

The children decide what could be done to cheer him up. Ask each child to suggest ways of making Charlie Bear feel better.

- *I'll brush him.*
- *I'll give him a cuddle.*
- *He could stay here with us.*

Collective drawing

Make a large group drawing of Charlie Bear.

- *I'll sew his ear back on.*
- *I'll give him a new squeaker.*
- *I'll tell him a joke.*
- *It doesn't matter about the new toys. You're still special.*

Narrate what happens to Charlie Bear depending on what the children have suggested. Perhaps he is mended and returns home, or maybe he stays at the workshop with the other toys.

Mime or still images

Let's pretend to be a floppy doll, a spinning top, or a cuddly rabbit. How would you stand? How would you move?

Activity 4   A new challenge for the apprentices

Teacher's intentions

- To set a new challenge.
- To encourage imagination about toy ideas and designs.

Drawings or models

Pictures or junk models of favourite toys.

Meeting: setting the task

Tell the children that Tonica the toymaker has gone on holiday and they are all in charge. While she is away, a visitor arrives at the workshop. Tell the children that you will take the role of the visitor:

Hello everyone. My name's Rupert. I work for a very large toy shop in the city. I've brought a letter from my boss. Shall I read it to you? [Read the letter (see p. 51).] As you can see, we are looking for people to make some toys for us for Christmas. We don't want electronic toys with batteries as we have enough of those already. We want old-fashioned, traditional toys made of wood and cloth and card. Would you be able to design and make some toys like this for us to sell? What do you think?

Discuss possibilities. Ask the children to show you around. Suggest they start making things as soon as possible.

Design and technology

Draw designs and make toys using the suggested materials.

Dramatic play: making the toys

The children get busy in the workshop, designing and making toys for Rupert through mimed activity. Props are not required. Rupert chats and makes suggestions while they work, reminding them about what he needs and what materials they can use.

Literacy

Put pictures of newly designed toys into a catalogue. Label the toys. Give them names and write a description to inform purchasers.

Design and technology

Use construction kits to make toys.

Meeting: how well did they do?

Teacher in role as Rupert invites the apprentices to gather together to show him the (imaginary) toys they have made.

- *Could you show me what you have designed/made for me?*
- *Hold it up so we can all see.*
- *What have you made? What tools did you use?*
- *Why will this be a good toy for children to have?*

Finally, he thanks them and tells them that he will write to Tonica when she returns, to tell her how good the apprentices all are.

Plenary

Discuss how the children helped the people they met in the drama.

- *Why did Tonica need their help?*
- *Why was Charlie Bear so sad?*
- *What advice did you offer him?*
- *How did you encourage him to talk to you when he was so shy?*
- *How did you help Rupert?*
- *Why do you think they didn't want any more electronic toys?*

• LINK TO •
'The Teddy Bears' Picnic' (Book 1) and 'Finders Keepers' (Book 3) for stories about teddy bears

• LINK TO •
'The Not So Jolly Postman' (Book 1), 'Mary Mary and the Giant' (Book 2) and 'The Lonely Dragon' (Book 3) for stories about helping others

© Jo Boulton and Judith Ackroyd (2004) *The Toymaker's Workshop and other stories*, David Fulton Publishers.

8 Beside the Seaside

The beach is a lovely place for children to come and play. The people who work there meet a number of different characters who have various problems to solve. Mai Ling is a little girl who is afraid of the water. Mal is looking after the donkeys for her sick uncle and needs help. Georgie is doing too much sunbathing and is getting very burnt. Let's hope the children can sort them out!

Aims

- To consider ways to solve problems.
- To encourage the use of different language registers.
- To develop prediction skills.

Themes

- The seaside.
- Helping others.
- Personal health and safety.
- Fears.

Resources

Optional

Costume suggestions: Mai Ling – swimming kit, goggles, towel, teddy, bucket and spade, arm bands or a rubber ring, shells; Mal – book about donkeys, bucket and shovel, old coat; Georgie – towel, suntan lotion, sunhat, bottle of water, T-shirt, sunglasses.

The imaginative play area can be designed as the beach or perhaps the travel agents.

Notes

In this drama we use a bag of clothing and props to introduce each new teacher role. This is a really good way to build up a picture of each character before the teacher 'becomes' them in the drama. It is important to choose a suitable bag for each role and carefully select a few appropriate items of clothing or props. Children are extremely good at reading signs; therefore be careful not to give a wrong impression of the role by choosing inappropriate clothing for it. You need to decide what impression you want the children to get and paint a clear picture so there is no confusion. For example, if you want Mal to be a more traditional older lady, perhaps choose a wicker basket and a shabby coat and a floral scarf rather than a plastic carrier-bag and a leather jacket. However, you may decide that Mal is a very trendy lady and would be very comfortable in a leather jacket and a motorbike helmet.

By revealing one thing from the bag at a time, suspense is built up and the children can offer their ideas about what they think the person is going to be like.

If you don't want to use props and costumes it is still possible to introduce the role by simply saying, 'In the next part of the story I am going to be Mai Ling.'

On the beach, by Charlie

Activity 1   The beach is a lovely place to work

Teacher's intentions

- To build investment in the beach.
- To develop individual roles.

Discussion: creating roles

Tell the children that you are going to tell them a story about a beach and they are going to be the people who work there. Decide what kinds of jobs the people would do. The children decide what jobs they would like to do on the beach (e.g. rent out deck-chairs to people on the beach, sell ice-creams, paint beach huts, do the Punch and Judy show). Make a list of jobs.

Stories
Read or tell stories about the beach. These could be anecdotal.

Still images and dramatic play: children work on the beach

Narrate:

One lovely day on the beach, all the people who worked there were working very hard.

- Ask them to find a space in the room and go to 'work'.
- Ask the children to freeze when you say 'one, two, three, Freeze', and show a still picture of jobs being done on the beach. This is like a postcard of a beach scene. The teacher walks round and talks to the children in turn about what they are doing.
- Bring the beach to life and wander around chatting to the people and finding out what's happening on the beach today. Encourage the children to make up their own stories and join in with their play.

Visit
Link this drama with a visit to the seaside or look at pictures of different beaches. What can we see, hear, smell, taste and touch at the seaside?

Discussion
Who has been on holiday?
Was it in this country or abroad?
Talk about day trips or holidays on the beach.
What do we know about the beach?
What might we find there?
Make a list (e.g. deck chairs, pier, beach huts, ice-cream stall, donkey rides).

Activity 2   Meeting Mai Ling

Teacher's intentions

- To introduce the teacher in role as Mai Ling.
- To be able to give comfort and reassurance.
- To be able to use persuasive language.

Discussion and creation of teacher in role: Mai Ling is introduced

Place the bag of props in the middle of the circle of seated children. Tell them that in the story about the beach today, they are going to meet someone new who has never been to the beach before. Her name is Mai Ling. She owns the bag in the middle and they are going to find out more about her by taking out one item at a time and seeing if they can make guesses about her, such as how old she is and what she likes doing.

Invite children one at a time to take items out of the bag and lay them on the floor. As each item of clothing or prop is removed from the bag, ask questions to draw out the children's understanding:

- *Why would she need a towel?*
- *What are the goggles used for?*
- *Why would she need arm bands?*
- *How old do you think she is?*

Tell the children that in the story you are going to be the little girl called Mai Ling who is about five years old. Arrange the props around you or hold some of them as appropriate. Tell the children that they are going to see Mai Ling and hear her speak but are not able to talk to her at the moment.

Teacher in role monologue: Mai Ling is scared

In role as Mai Ling, sit down, holding the teddy tightly, and look around you nervously.

Oh dear. I've never been to the beach before. It's so big. My brothers and sisters have gone off down to the sea for a swim but I'm too scared. They say it's fun but I don't think so at all. It looks cold and wet and there are scary waves to knock me over. And I don't like the sand. It sticks to my feet.

Discussion and hot seating: how can we help her?

Put down the teddy and talk to the children as teacher. What have they heard? Why is Mai Ling looking so upset? What could the people who work on the beach say to her to cheer her up and give her confidence?

The workers talk to Mai Ling about her worries. They try to reassure her that things are not really scary, but exciting and fun. They can also give her advice about keeping safe on the beach (e.g. not going into the water on her own or when the waves are big).

Whole group improvisation: looking around the beach

The workers could show Mai Ling around the beach and introduce themselves. They could lead her down to the water's edge and teach her to paddle or jump over the waves.

- *I'm worried I might fall into the water and drown.*
- *Why is the sea so big?*
- *I'm frightened about what I might tread on.*
- *What are these empty shell things for?*

They could show her how to skim stones across the water or build a sandcastle.

- *How do you make sure the sand sticks together to make a castle?*
- *I haven't got a flag. What else could I stick on the top?*

They could also teach her about the dangers of the sea and how to stay safe.

- *Should I just run straight in?*
- *I could lie down and let the sea cover me up. Would I be able to breathe?*

After a while Mai Ling thanks the workers for their help and says she feels much better now. She is happy to play on the edge and wait for her family without feeling nervous and knowing how to stay safe.

Knowledge and understanding/ science

Why do we use towels to dry ourselves? Think about using different types of material to dry yourself after swimming. Experiment with the absorption of different materials.

Plenary discussion: what did Mai Ling learn?

Talk about Mai Ling and what the children thought of her.

- *Was she a nice person?*
- *Why had she come to the beach?*
- *What did you help her to do?*
- *What did she learn?*
- *What could she do now – learn to swim?*

Collective drawing

Children draw an individual picture of something they would like to see on the beach or a picture of themselves working or playing on the beach. These may be stuck on to a large sheet of paper to create a collective montage. Use a digital camera to take pictures of the children's faces. These may be stuck on to the children's self-portraits so that everyone can appear in the collective picture.

Geography

Look at a map and identify different beaches. Put flags on the map to indicate where the children have visited. Talk about and identify other geographical features identified on maps that are found on beaches (e.g. caves, rivers, swamps, sand-dunes).

Activity 3   Meeting Mal

Teacher's intentions

- To introduce a new teacher role with a new problem.
- To use the children's knowledge to solve the problem.

Discussion and creation of new teacher role: meeting Mal

Place the next bag of props in the middle of the circle of seated children. Tell the children that in the story about the beach today, they are going to meet another person whom they have never met before. This person owns the bag in the middle and they are going to find out more about the person by taking out one item at a time and seeing if they can guess who it is going to be this time.

As before, invite the children one at a time to take items out of the bag and lay them on the floor. As each item of clothing or prop is removed, ask questions to draw out the children's understandings.

Tell the children that in the story you are going to be in role as the person who owns these things. Dress in the clothes or hold the props as you choose. Ask the children to give the person a name – we will call her Mal.

Tell them that you will be Mal and she will be arriving in a few minutes.

Teacher in role and whole group improvisation: Mal needs some help

Children in role as beach workers are approached by teacher in role as Mal and begin a conversation. Mal is a lively, jolly lady who is in a spot of bother. Her uncle is Mr Atkins who owns the donkeys and he has been taken ill. She has come down to the beach to look after the donkeys and run the donkey ride business but isn't sure what to do. She's never looked after any animals before. Can they help her by advising how to feed, groom and exercise the donkeys? If appropriate, a book on animals could be used to access information about correct approaches, but as long as the ideas are reasonable it is probably better to accept the children's suggestions. Mal asks for their help to look after the donkeys. This can be achieved through mime or improvisation.

- *Can you show me how to brush this donkey?*
- *Should I do it like this? Is this right?*
- *What do I need this bucket and shovel for?*

Plenary discussion: how did we help Mal?

Talk about Mal and what they thought of her.

- *Was she a busy person?*
- *Why had she come to the beach?*
- *What did you help her to do?*

Activity 4   Meeting Georgie

Teacher's intentions

- To develop the children's roles.
- To interact with a different teacher in role.
- To give advice and guidance to the teacher in role.
- To use argument, giving alternatives, listening to alternative viewpoints.
- To raise issues about safety in the sun.

Discussion and creation of final teacher role: meeting Georgie

Place the next bag of props in the middle of the circle of seated children. Tell the children that in the story about the beach today they are going to meet another person whom they have never met before. This person owns the bag in the middle and they are going to find out more about the person by taking out one item at a time.

As before, invite the children one at a time to take items out of the bag and lay them on the floor. As each item of clothing or prop is removed, ask questions to draw out the children's understanding.

Tell the children that in the story you are going to be the person who owns these things. Dress in the clothes or hold the props as you choose. Ask the children to give the person a name – we will call the person Georgie. They can be male or female. Tell them that you will be Georgie and will be arriving in a few minutes. They are to watch what happens and then will talk about what they have seen Georgie do.

Teacher in role monologue: Georgie is feeling ill

Unroll the towel and lie down. Fan your face. Sigh. Shuffle around as if feeling uncomfortable.

The sun's really hot today. I've been lying here for hours. I am feeling really strange. My skin is burning and I've got a headache. I wonder why I'm feeling like this. I'm really thirsty but I didn't bring a drink with me. I feel sick.

Discussion: what is wrong with Georgie?

Why is Georgie feeling bad? Try to get the children to tell you about the dangers of being out in the sun for too long and what you need to do to prevent dehydration and burning. Georgie has all the necessary clothing and equipment in the bag and the children will hopefully refer to the hat, the water and the suntan lotion. Tell the children that they are going to have the chance to speak to Georgie about it.

Art
Use sea colours to paint seascapes. Mix paint and sand to lend texture to paintings.

Design
Children can design a selection of beachwear for themselves (e.g. a towel, a sunhat, a swimsuit, sunglasses, a beach bag).

Water safety
Make a poster about safety in the water.

Science/ knowledge and understanding
Identify, draw and label creatures that can be found on the beach (e.g. crabs, seagulls, creatures with shells).

Whole group improvisation and teacher in role: giving advice to Georgie

Hello everyone. I wonder if you could help me. I'm feeling a bit poorly. I've been sunbathing for a few hours and I want to get a good tan. Wearing a hat is silly. Mum gave me this one and I feel stupid. If I put cream on I won't tan so quickly. I've heard people say 'Slip, slap, slop.' I've wondered what it meant. Do you know?

Workers offer advice to Georgie about ways to avoid burning by wearing a hat and a T-shirt and to avoid headaches by drinking water.

Plenary discussion

Talk about Georgie and what the workers thought about the sunbathing.

- *What advice did you give?*
- *Did you change Georgie's point of view?*

Knowledge and understanding/science and geography

Talk about erosion and how the sea erodes the coastline. Look at different pebbles and talk about the way the sea has rubbed them into smooth shapes. Look at sand grains and discuss how sand is formed.

• LINK TO •

'The Lost Hat' (Book 1) and 'The Toymaker's Workshop' and 'Humpty Dumpty' (Book 3) for stories about helping others

• LINK TO •

'The Health Centre' (Book 1) and 'In the Jungle' (Book 2) for health issues

• LINK TO •

'The Not So Jolly Postman' (Book 1), 'Mary Mary and the Giant' (Book 2) and 'The Lonely Dragon' (Book 3) for stories about confronting fears

9 Billy Goats Gruff

The Billy Goats Gruff have always lived to the east of the river. They have fed well on the lush grass. However, as they look over the bridge, they are sure that the grass to the west of the river is even greener and lusher. The only trouble is that a horrible troll lives under the bridge and stops anyone trying to cross it. The smallest goat mounts the bridge first. He avoids being eaten by the troll since he promises that his brother will be tastier to eat. The second goat does the same and the troll awaits his big breakfast of the third goat. However, the largest goat is pretty tough himself, and butts the troll over the bridge and into the river. He is never seen again and the goats cross the bridge when they please.

Aims

- To explore a traditional tale.
- To discuss greed, and why people are greedy and selfish.
- To consider ways of resolving conflict.

Themes

- Traditional tales.
- Greed and selfishness.
- Bullying.

Resources

Optional: Different items of clothing for the three Billy Goats and the troll.

Large sheets of sugar paper joined to make a very large sheet, or a long length of wallpaper; coloured markers.

The imaginative play area can be designed as Fairy-tale Land.

Activity 1   Setting the scene and imagining the troll

Teacher's intentions

- To start the story.
- To share an image of the troll.
- To work as a group on one large drawing.

Introduction: narration

The three Billy Goats Gruff have always lived to the east of the river. They have fed well on the lush grass. However, as they look over the bridge, they are sure that the grass to the west of the river is even greener and lusher. The only trouble is that a horrible troll lives under the bridge and stops anyone trying to cross it.

Discuss with the class what they have heard so far:

- *How many Billy Goats Gruff are there?*
- *Whereabouts do they live?*
- *What bothers them?*
- *What is a troll?*

Collective drawing: creating the troll

Join large sheets of sugar paper together or unroll a long length of wallpaper, blank side up. Draw a huge head and body. These could be two circles or oval shapes that fill most of the paper. Invite children to make suggestions about what the troll looks like. They can take it in turns to add aspects of the troll, such as eyes and horns. They may want it to have big teeth and warts on its face. As features are discussed and agreed upon, they are added to the drawing:

- *What is it about the troll that makes it look frightening?*
- *What might its ears look like?*
- *Are its legs thick or thin? Are they knobbly or smooth?*

Invite words to describe the troll the children have created. Write them around the picture.

Activity 2   Why won't the troll let anyone cross the bridge?

Teacher's intentions

- To move the story on.
- To provide an opportunity for the children to meet the troll.

Hot seating: questioning the troll

- *Why do you think that the troll might not let anyone pass?*
- *Why does he live under the bridge?*

Explain that you will play the part of the troll so that the children can ask him what he is up to. Ask them how you should sit as the troll and what sort of voice you might have. You could put the picture on the floor in front of a chair. When you sit on that chair you are the troll. Don't forget to leave the chair before you begin to speak as the teacher again. The troll is not very nice. Answer questions as might the pantomime villain.

I like living under the bridge because it means I can trap anyone who walks by. My tummy is never very full. I love to eat anything that comes over the bridge. I love to see all the animals and humans scared of me. It makes me laugh. This is my bridge. I live here. I don't like any noise when I am sleeping under <u>MY</u> bridge. If I hear someone on my bridge, I roar out, 'Who's that trip-trapping over my bridge?'

Ordering sizes

Place objects in order of size. Use scales to place objects in order of weight.

Create a model environment

Create a large three-dimensional model of the scene with grass banks, a river, the bridge, the troll and the three goats.

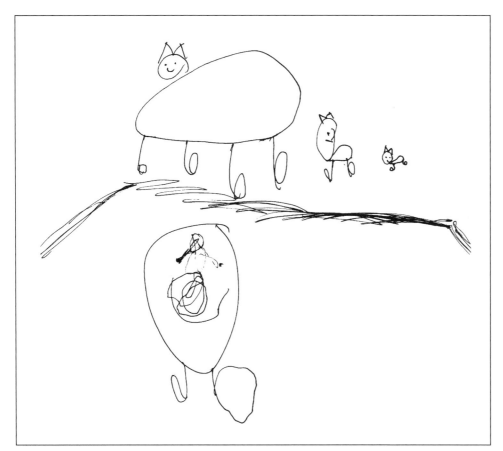

Billy Goats Gruff, by Charlie

© Jo Boulton and Judith Ackroyd (2004) *The Toymaker's Workshop and other stories*, David Fulton Publishers.

Activity 3   The goats and the bridge

Geography

Where do goats live? What do they require for survival? Why are they reared?

Teacher's intentions

- To consider the perspective of the goats.
- To practise using the repeated phrase from the story.
- To create the bridge.

Physically creating: making the bridge

The children can create the bridge and practise the roar of the troll.

Arrange the children in two rows opposite each other about a metre apart. The idea is to create the arc shape of the bridge by the height of the children. Those at either end kneel down to be the parts of the bridge nearest the bank. The next few towards the centre kneel up to indicate the slight rise of the bridge. The next few in at either end sit on chairs, while those nearest the middle stand up.

The children can then practise booming out in role as the troll, *'Who's that trip-trapping over my bridge?'* This bridge and the roar are returned to very soon in the drama.

Narration, discussion: the goats want to cross the bridge

The goats have spent some time looking at the other side of the river. Why do they want to cross to the other side of the bridge? Are there any other reasons they may wish to cross over beyond the grass?

Examples are: they have friends over there; they are bored with the same place and like to explore.

The goats talk about getting to the other side. In the end it is the smallest goat that mounts the bridge first. He says he will not be eaten. He has an idea! He will tell the troll to let him pass, and not to eat him since his brother who is passing over the bridge soon is much fatter and will be tastier to eat.

It is important to provide this detail before asking a child to play the goat so that s/he knows what to say.

Growing grass

Plant grass seed in pots. The children can water it and then trim the grass with scissors. See how quickly the grass grows if you put some pots in sunny places and others in shady corners. Do pots near the window grow more quickly than those in darker places? Which seem to use more water? Is there any difference in the colour of the grass? Which would the goats like best? Look at grass outside and find sunny places and shady places under tall trees.

Activity 4 Crossing the bridge

Teacher's intentions

- To move to the climax of the story.
- To meet the troll.

Creating the bridge and thought tracking: the little billy goat's attempt

Form the bridge again as in Activity 3 and invite a child to be the little billy goat. *How will the little billy goat be feeling at this moment?* He is frightened, but thinks he should try to look brave. He isn't sure that he will make it to the other side. He approaches the bridge.

Ask the child to approach the bridge very slowly and then to move between the children who form the sides of the bridge. Ask the children at the edges of the bridge to say what they think the billy goat would be thinking as he steps slowly over the bridge. What will the troll look like? *Will the troll eat me? Should I run back?*

Tell the children making up the bridge that when you appear in role as the troll at the end of the bridge, they must all roar, *'Who's that trip-trapping over my bridge?'*

Tell the little goat that you will eat him up. S/he will reply that the big brother will be juicier and so on. Take a while to be convinced before letting the little goat pass.

Repeat this action with another child who plays the second billy goat (the first child returns to their place in the bridge). The thoughts are spoken again and the troll roars. The troll may be harder to persuade this time. Then narrate what has taken place:

The little billy goat avoids being eaten by the troll since he promises that his brother will be tastier to eat. The second troll does the same and the troll awaits his large, juicy breakfast of the biggest billy goat of all. However, the largest goat is pretty tough himself, and butts the troll over the bridge and into the river.

A third child becomes the big billy goat who approaches the bridge. The thoughts as he approaches may be different this time: *My brothers got over all right, so why shouldn't I? No troll will stop me doing what I want! I want that yummy grass on the other side of the bridge.*

Again the troll appears and the children roar. The troll says he will eat the billy goat, but the big billy goat is not afraid and charges at the troll, who should quickly move around the end of the bridge and run away.

From that day on, the troll is never seen again and the goats cross the bridge when they please.

Sink or float?

The troll sinks into the river and is never seen again. What other objects might sink? Experiment with bowls of water and a range of objects. Make lists of objects which float and objects which sink.

Soundscape

Children in groups make appropriate sounds for different parts of the story. Examples include: *Tell the story and bring in the sounds*. Children particularly enjoy the trip-trapping sound of hooves on a wooden bridge.

Literacy

Discuss story language. How do fairy-tales often begin? (e.g. Once upon a time, long ago). Discuss other vocabulary from this story such as lush, billy goat and gruff.

Activity 5   Plenary: reflection and discussion

Teacher's intentions

- To evaluate tactics for problem-solving.
- To consider the danger of listening to rumour.

Gossip-mongers

The animals in the area were very excited that they could now cross the bridge whenever they liked. They told each other stories of how the Billy Goats Gruff had got rid of the troll. Some of the stories were a little exaggerated. Some told of bigger arguments and shouts and fights. They described the troll in different ways, too.

Children take turns to tell bits of exaggerated stories: *The big billy goat spun the troll around in the air fifty times before throwing him in the river!*

Why would the animals exaggerate?

Consider a range of questions

- *Was the little billy goat any less successful than the big billy goat?*
- *How were their tactics different?*
- *How else might they have stopped the troll controlling the bridge?*

Internet stories

Different versions of the story can be downloaded from the internet:
www.surlalunefairytales.com/billygoats/story.
www.sterlingtimes.co.uk/bill_goats_gruff.html (this site provides a song).
www.pitt_edu/-dash/ type0122e.html (includes versions from Norway, Poland and Germany).

Possibilities are tried out (e.g. the goats could explain to the troll that everybody is afraid of him and he is spoiling their lives, or they may try to persuade him that being selfish and greedy does not make you popular with others). The teacher in role as troll may just laugh, or may wish to admit that he is lonely since he has no friends and invite the goats and their friends to cross the bridge as they please. He may need to think what he will eat instead!

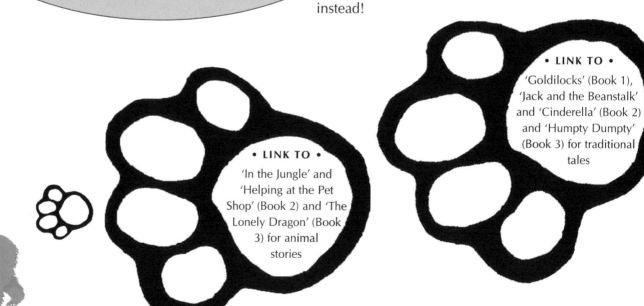

• LINK TO •
'In the Jungle' and 'Helping at the Pet Shop' (Book 2) and 'The Lonely Dragon' (Book 3) for animal stories

• LINK TO •
'Goldilocks' (Book 1), 'Jack and the Beanstalk' and 'Cinderella' (Book 2) and 'Humpty Dumpty' (Book 3) for traditional tales

Finders Keepers

Avina is playing in the play-park with her friends until it is time for the park to close. Just as she is about to set off for home on her scooter, she sees something lying under the swing, partly hidden by grass. When she investigates she finds a teddy bear which has been left by one of the children. She decides to take it home with her. At first she is really pleased with her new toy. However, when her friends tell her that the little boy who has lost the teddy is very sad, she has to make a difficult decision.

Aims

- To consider personal responsibility.
- To discuss right and wrong.
- To create opportunities for a range of different speaking registers.
- To recognise that there are choices to be made.

Themes

- Fair and unfair.
- Right and wrong.
- Moral development.
- Toys.

Resources

A teddy bear.
Optional: A simple prop such as a scarf to indicate when you are in role.

The imaginative play area can be designed as the park, the playground or the café (see Book 1).

Notes

The idea for this drama came from the books *Jamaica's Find* by Juanita Havill and *Dogger* by Shirley Hughes.

The setting for this drama can be changed from the park to anything suitable that fits in with your theme (e.g. a nursery, school playground, after-school club, beach or café).

The play-park is the term we use to describe the play area in the park where there are swings, slides, climbing frame, see-saw and so on.

When asking children to be in role as children this can sometimes cause difficulties, since they will tend to pretend to be younger than they are and revert to babyish behaviour. We find it useful to stress that the children in *this* story are older than the chronological age of the actual children in the group and are in fact quite grown-up!

Eating ice-cream at the park, by Charlie

Activity 1   At the play-park

Teacher's intentions

- To introduce the context for the drama.
- To develop listening skills.
- To introduce the teacher role of Avina.
- To use mime and dramatic play to build belief in the setting and characters.

Still images: setting the scene

Tell the children that you are going to tell a story about some children who like to go to the play-park at the weekend with their friends. Discuss who goes to such places and what they like about them. Discuss what equipment would be in the play-park (e.g. swings, slide, climbing frame). Ask groups of children to stand in designated spaces: *'This is the roundabout.' 'This is the see-saw.'* Ask the children to make a still image of the children playing in the park on a sunny day. Look at each image in turn and bring each one to life for a few seconds.

Dramatic play: playing in the park

When all the images have been seen, narrate:

One sunny afternoon all the children were playing in the park. Some were on the swings, some were eating ice-creams. It was a lovely day.

Then bring the park to life. Tell the children that they can move from one activity to another and they can also mime playing football, Frisbee throwing and so on.

Go around chatting and asking questions about what is happening. This can go on for as long as the children are engaged in the activity.

Stories…
About toys: *Old Bear Stories* by Jane Hissey; *Dogger* by Shirley Hughes; *Jamaica's Find* by Juanita Havill.

Activity 2   Avina arrives at the play-park

Teacher's intentions

● To introduce the teacher in role.

● To practise using descriptive language.

Discussion with teacher in role: a new girl arrives

Tell the children that they are going to meet someone who is new to the park and you are going to be that person. The children in the park are having a rest and a drink when the new girl arrives. What will they say to her? Will they want to ask her any questions?

Walk away from the children and use a prop to show when you are in role. Avina is a shy girl, desperate to be friends with the children. Try not to talk too much to begin with, as the children may need encouragement to ask questions.

Hello everyone. [Wait for them to respond.]

The following information can be given in response to the children's questions.

My name is Avina. I'm ten years old. I've just moved into the area. I haven't got any brothers or sisters. I'm going to go to the school just over there. Is that where you go? What are the teachers like? Is there a playground? Do you play football at break? This is a great park. Could you tell me what there is to do here? Could you show me around?

At the play-park, by Charlie

© Jo Boulton and Judith Ackroyd (2004) *The Toymaker's Workshop and other stories*, David Fulton Publishers.

Activity 3   Avina has a dilemma

Teacher's intentions

- To encourage empathy with a character.
- To introduce a moral dilemma.

Teacher in role, monologue and mimed action: I've found something

Tell the children that it is time for everyone to go home for tea and Avina is left in the park alone.

I'll just have one last go on the swing. Oh what's this? It's a teddy. Oh it's really cute.

Look around as if to see whether you are being watched.

Discussion: what should she do?

Ask the children how they think that Avina is feeling at the moment. What is she going to do with the teddy? What choices does she have?

Conscience alley: giving advice to Avina

Ask the children to make a path for Avina to walk along as if she was walking to the park gate. As she passes each of them they can tell her what they think she should do with the teddy and why.

Finish with:

Avina put the teddy under her coat and took it home. Finders keepers, losers weepers.

Personal, social and emotional development

Use a circle-time activity to think about naughty things that hands can do and the good things that hands can do.

Activity 4   It's my bear now

Teacher's intentions

- To use persuasive language.
- To discuss right and wrong and fairness.
- To focus on the choices people make and how this can impact on others.

Discussion with teacher in role

Tell the children that Avina took the teddy home and went to her bedroom. It is good if you can act this out with the children observing you, or you could narrate what happens.

I'd better play with it here or Mum will see. She'll want to know where the teddy came from.

You are my first ever teddy. Come on teddy, meet my other toys. You're mine now.

Play with the teddy for a while, then put it on a chair and look at it.

Look directly at the children watching you and address them:

I feel really funny inside. Why do I feel like that? Do you know?

Hopefully they will respond to Avina, telling her that she shouldn't have taken the teddy or that she should take it back tomorrow.

Her argument is:

- The person shouldn't have left it there in the first place.
- They clearly don't love the teddy as much as she does because she'd never leave it in the park.
- Finders keepers.
- She doesn't know the children very well yet so it doesn't matter if she upsets any of them.

The children may manage to persuade her that she has been wrong and that she will feel better if she returns the teddy to the park tomorrow.

Literacy – for and against

Write a list of the reasons why Avina should keep the teddy and a list of why she should not keep it.

Consequences

Think about the consequences of different actions.
If I hit someone I will . . .
If I am hit by someone . . .
If I steal something . . .
If I tell a lie . . .

Activity 5 Avina returns the teddy

Teacher's intentions

- To go through the process of owning up to something.
- To provide a positive ending.

Conscience alley: I know I've been wrong

Explain to the children that the following morning Avina goes back to the park with the teddy.

We are going to find out how she is feeling as she is walking back along the path towards the play-park where all the children are playing.

The children speak Avina's thoughts at this point in the story as the teacher in role walks up the path:

- *I'm worried.*
- *They might not like me any more.*
- *I'll feel better when I've given it back.*
- *I bet the teddy's real owner is feeling sad.*

As soon as you reach the end of the alley turn around and address the children in role as Avina:

Hello. Last night I found this teddy by the swings. I took it home with me because I liked it and wanted to keep it. But I felt so bad because it belongs to one of you and you are my new friends. I'm sorry.

It is then up to the children how they respond to Avina's confession!

Plenary discussion

- Why did Avina take the teddy in the first place?
- How did she feel when she was in her bedroom?
- How did the children react to her?
- What will happen in the future? Will they all be friends?
- Why is it always best to own up when you have done something naughty?

Collections
Favourite toys, books about toys.

Emotions
Discuss Avina's different emotions throughout the story. How did she feel at the beginning? How did she feel at the end? When was she scared? When was she embarrassed?

Personal, social and emotional development
Use circle time to talk about how we feel if we do something wrong. Talk about emotions such as embarrassment and guilt. Talk about the physical symptoms we have such as blushing, knotted stomach, butterflies. Talk about doing the right thing and how that makes us feel.

• LINK TO •
'The Lost Hat' and 'Goldilocks' (Book 1) and 'Pirate Adventure' (Book 2) for stories about respecting the property of others

• LINK TO •
'The Park' (Book 1) for the imaginative play area

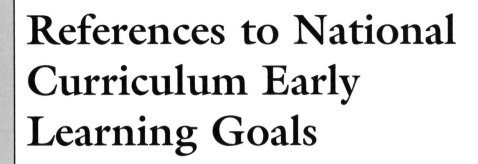

References to National Curriculum Early Learning Goals

EARLY LEARNING GOALS

	CHAPTER									
	1	2	3	4	5	6	7	8	9	10
Personal, social and emotional development										
1 Continue to be interested, excited and motivated to learn.	•	•	•	•	•	•	•	•	•	•
2 Be confident to try new activities, initiate ideas and speak in a familiar group.	•	•	•	•	•	•	•	•	•	•
3 Maintain attention, concentrate, and sit quietly when appropriate.	•	•	•	•	•	•	•	•	•	•
4 Respond to significant experiences, showing a range of feelings when appropriate.	•	•	•	•	•	•	•	•	•	•
5 Have a developing awareness of their own needs, views and feelings and be sensitive to the needs, views and feelings of others.	•	•	•	•	•	•	•	•	•	•
7 Form good relationships with adults and peers.	•	•	•	•	•	•	•	•	•	•
8 Work as part of a group or class, taking turns and sharing fairly; understand that there need to be agreed values and codes of behaviour for groups of people, including adults and children, to work together harmoniously.	•	•	•	•	•	•	•			
9 Understand what is right, what is wrong, and why.	•	•	•	•	•	•	•	•	•	•
10 Consider the consequences of their words and actions for themselves and others.	•	•	•	•	•	•	•	•	•	•
13 Understand that people have different needs, views, cultures and beliefs that need to be treated with respect.	•	•	•	•	•	•	•	•	•	•
14 Understand that they can expect others to treat their needs, views, cultures and beliefs with respect.	•	•	•	•	•	•	•	•	•	•

EARLY LEARNING GOALS

	CHAPTER									
	1	2	3	4	5	6	7	8	9	10
Communication, language and literacy										
1 Interact with others, negotiating plans and activities and taking turns in conversation.	•	•	•	•	•	•	•	•	•	•
2 Enjoy listening to and using spoken and written language, and readily turn to it in their play and learning.	•	•	•	•	•	•	•	•	•	•
3 Sustain attentive listening responding to what they have heard by relevant comments, questions or actions.	•	•	•	•	•	•	•	•	•	•
4 Listen with enjoyment, and respond to stories, songs and other music, rhymes and poems and make up their own stories, songs, rhymes and poems.	•	•	•	•	•	•	•	•	•	•
5 Extend vocabulary, exploring the meanings and sounds of new words.	•	•	•	•	•	•	•	•	•	•
6 Speak clearly and audibly with confidence and control and show awareness of the listener, for example by their use of conventions such as greetings.	•	•	•	•	•	•	•	•	•	•
7 Use language to imagine and re-create roles and experiences.	•	•	•	•	•	•	•	•	•	•
8 Use talk to organise, sequence and clarify thinking, ideas, feelings and events.	•	•	•	•	•	•	•	•	•	•
13 Retell narratives in the correct sequence, drawing on language patterns of stories.	•	•	•	•	•	•	•	•	•	•
16 Show an understanding of the elements of stories, such as main character, sequence of events, and answer questions about where, who, why and when.	•	•	•	•	•	•	•	•	•	•

EARLY LEARNING GOALS

	CHAPTER									
	1	2	3	4	5	6	7	8	9	10
Knowledge and understanding of the world										
2 Find out about, and identify, some features of living things, objects and events which they observe.						•				
4 Ask questions about why things happen and how things work.			•		•		•			
5 Build and construct with a wide range of objects, selecting appropriate resources, and adapting their work where necessary.			•				•		•	
9 Observe, find out and identify features in the place they live and the natural world.			•	•	•			•		
10 Find out about their environment and talk about those features they like and dislike.			•	•	•			•		
Physical development										
1 Move with confidence, imagination and in safety.	•	•	•	•	•	•	•	•	•	•
2 Move with control and coordination.	•	•	•	•	•	•	•		•	•
4 Show awareness of space, of themselves and of others.	•	•	•	•	•	•	•	•	•	•
Creative development										
3 Use their imagination in art and design, music, dance, imaginative and role play and stories.	•	•	•	•	•	•	•	•	•	•
5 Express and communicate their ideas, thoughts and feelings by using . . . imaginative and role play . . . movement.	•	•	•	•	•	•	•	•	•	•

NATIONAL CURRICULUM KEY STAGE 1

	CHAPTER									
	1	2	3	4	5	6	7	8	9	10
En1 Speaking and Listening										
1 Speaking										
a speak clear diction and use appropriate intonation	•	•	•	•	•	•	•	•	•	•
b choose words with precision	•	•	•	•	•	•	•	•	•	•
c organise what they say	•	•	•	•	•	•	•	•	•	•
d focus on the main points	•	•	•	•	•	•	•	•	•	•
e include relevant detail	•	•	•	•	•	•	•	•	•	•
f take into account the needs of the listener	•	•	•	•	•	•	•	•	•	•
2 Listening										
a sustain concentration	•	•	•	•	•	•	•	•	•	•
b remember specific points that interest them	•	•	•	•	•	•	•	•	•	•
c make relevant comments	•	•	•	•	•	•	•	•	•	•
d listen to others' reactions	•	•	•	•	•	•	•	•	•	•
e ask questions to clarify their understanding	•	•	•	•	•	•	•	•	•	
f identify and respond to sound patterns in language						•				
3 Group discussion and interaction										
a take turns in speaking	•	•	•	•	•	•	•	•	•	•
b relate their contribution to what has gone before	•	•	•	•	•	•	•	•	•	•
c take different views into account	•	•	•	•	•	•	•	•	•	•
d extend their ideas in the light of discussion	•	•	•	•	•	•	•	•	•	•
e give reasons for opinions and actions	•	•	•	•	•	•	•	•	•	•

NATIONAL CURRICULUM KEY STAGE 1

	CHAPTER									
	1	2	3	4	5	6	7	8	9	10
4 Drama										
a use language and actions to explore and convey situations, characters and emotions	•	•	•	•	•	•	•	•	•	•
b create and sustain roles individually and when working with others	•	•	•	•	•	•	•	•	•	•
c comment constructively on drama they have watched or in which they have taken part	•	•	•	•	•	•	•	•	•	•
6 Language variation										
a pupils should be taught how speech varies in different circumstances	•	•	•	•	•	•	•	•	•	•
b to take account of different listeners	•	•	•	•	•	•	•	•	•	•
Sc2 Science										
2b humans and other animals need food and water to stay alive	•			•				•		
3a to recognise that plants need light and water to grow					•					
b to recognise and name the leaf, flower, stem and root of flowering plants					•					
4a to recognise similarities and differences between ourselves and others, and to treat others with sensitivity					•	•		•		
5c to care for the environment					•					
Geography										
2a use geographical vocabulary					•			•		
e make maps and plans			•		•			•		
3a identify and describe what places are like	•		•	•	•			•	•	

NATIONAL CURRICULUM KEY STAGE 1

	CHAPTER									
	1	2	3	4	5	6	7	8	9	10
PSHE and Citizenship										
1a to recognise what they like and dislike, what is fair and unfair, and what is right and wrong	•	•	•	•	•	•	•	•	•	•
b to share their opinions on things that matter to them and explain their views	•	•	•	•	•	•	•	•	•	•
c to recognise, name and deal with their feelings in a positive way	•	•	•	•	•	•	•	•	•	•
2a to take part in discussions with one other person and the whole class	•	•	•	•	•	•	•	•	•	•
c to recognise choices they can make, and recognise the difference between right and wrong	•	•	•	•	•	•	•	•	•	•
d to agree and follow rules for their group and classroom and understand how rules help them	•	•	•	•	•	•		•		•
e to recognise that people and other living things have needs, and that they have responsibilities to meet them	•	•	•	•	•	•	•	•	•	•
g what improves and harms their local, natural and built environments and about some of the ways people look after them	•		•		•			•		
3a how to make simple choices that improve their health and well-being										
f that all household products, including medicine, can be harmful if not used properly						•				
4a to recognise how their behaviour affects other people	•	•	•	•	•	•	•	•	•	•
b to listen to other people, and play and work cooperatively	•	•	•	•	•	•	•	•	•	•
c to identify and respect the differences and similarities between people	•	•	•	•	•	•	•	•	•	•
d that family and friends should care for each other	•	•	•	•	•	•	•		•	•
e that there are different types of teasing and bullying, that bullying is wrong, and how to get help to deal with bullying	•							•	•	

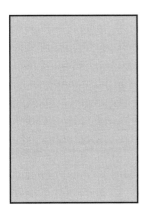

Glossary

This glossary of dramatic terms is not necessary to teach the activities in the foregoing chapters. Each activity is fully explained. However, a glossary providing explanations of a range of the dramatic approaches used in the book may help those who, having used them in these dramas, wish to plan their own drama sessions.

Conscience alley or thought tunnel

This invites children to examine a moment in the drama in detail. It is employed most effectively when a decision has to be made, or when a decision has already been irrevocably made. Sometimes it requires the children to offer advice to a character, too. Children consider what they or the character might think about the decision and its implications.

The children stand in two lines facing each other about a metre apart. The teacher walks very slowly from one end of the 'alley' to the other. As she does so, she turns to the child to one side and then the other. They speak aloud a word or a line (e.g. to Goldilocks, *'You should leave this cottage'*).

The thought tunnel offers a way of speaking a character's thoughts, rather than giving advice. The character moves through the tunnel in exactly the same way.

Alleys or tunnels can be curved to represent the context, such as a winding path, but straight lines enable children to see and hear each other better.

Discussion in role

Here the teacher is in role as well as the children while they discuss an issue or problem. The conversation is not *about* the characters (e.g. *What do you think frightens him?*) but *between* the characters (e.g. *Do you understand why I am frightened?*). The meeting takes place *as if* the teacher and children are other people in another place; in a fictional context. Discussion in role may be set up as a formal meeting held to sort out problems or discuss plans.

Dramatic construction

We have used this term to describe moments when the children physically 'become' something inanimate. They become a bridge in 'Billy Goats Gruff' (Book 3) and a fish tank in 'Helping at the Pet Shop' (Book 2). It may be used to set the scene for action as in the former, or to introduce terms and understand a structure as in the latter.

Dramatic play

Here children are indulging in imaginative play, but in the context of the shared drama.

They may be preparing some food, making a toy or painting a rocket. The action is not controlled by the teacher, but the teacher may wander among the children asking them about what they are doing as though she, too, is involved in the fiction: *'What flavour is your cake going to be?', 'How will you make that?', 'How did you reach to paint that top bit?'*

The children have freedom for individual creativity and are involved in their own worlds, so that while one is baking a cake in the kitchen another is shopping for drinks. High levels of concentration or emotion are not necessary in dramatic play, though of course they may occur. The activity helps to build up belief in the fiction.

Hot seating

The teacher is usually the best person to have in a hot seat since the pressure can be high. The device is helpful as a way to give information to children without being 'the teacher'. The children can ask questions directly to a character in a hot seat to find out whatever they wish to know. This requires them to find the most appropriate questions and sometimes the best way to ask them. The children might ask as themselves or in role as others in the drama.

Meeting

This highly structured activity engages the teacher and children together in role, gathered for a specific purpose. This may be to hear new information, make plans or discuss strategies. The teacher will usually be the chair or leader at the meeting so that she can order the proceedings and ensure all children's views are heard. Formal meetings are enhanced by an arrangement of chairs or benches in appropriate rows, and perhaps an agreed action when the chair enters the room. Decisions about pace and procedures will depend upon the context of the meeting.

Narration and narration with mimed action

Teacher narration in drama activities is a useful strategy for setting the scene or moving the action along. It is often a very useful controlling device! The teacher is empowered to dictate particular aspects of the drama. A class working noisily, for example, may hear the teacher narrate, *'Gradually, they fell silent. The helpers were too tired to speak.'* Narration is also used to excite interest and build tension in the drama (e.g. *'No one knew what was inside the bag. Some wondered if it might contain secrets while others felt sure it contained the lost treasure.'*). It may be used to set the scene (e.g. *'The hall was enormous and richly decorated'*) and to move the action forward (e.g. *'They all packed their bags and started the dangerous journey'*).

We enjoy drawing the children into narration through mimed action. *'The villagers had to climb up over high rocks'* on a journey, for example, would be accompanied by everyone miming climbing over imaginary rocks. It may also be used to help the children to imagine they are all one character (e.g. *'She put on her big strong boots, tying the laces tightly. She then put on a heavy coat and did up the buttons, one, two, three and four.'*). Each child, in his own space, will mime the actions as the teacher narrates.

Ritual

Ritual is a repeated procedure that those involved give value to, and are familiar with. In drama a ritual is used to give action significance. Any action, no matter how mundane, may be performed in a formal and dignified manner to make the actions seem to matter. Putting items into a picnic basket, for example, by having one child at a time step forward to place an imaginary contribution into the basket announcing what it is, brings about a more serious level of thought to the action and a more exciting atmosphere.

Statementing

Statementing involves the children literally in making statements about a person, event or place in the drama. The statements may be made in a ritualistic manner, with children stepping forward one at a time to voice their statement. They may remain frozen in a gesture appropriate to the statement while others make their statements, or they may return to their original place and watch the others. It is a way of involving children in the construction of events or characters so that they have a sense of ownership.

Still images and still image building

To make still images, children arrange themselves as though they are in a three-dimensional picture, depicting a scene or a particular moment. It creates a frozen moment when we imagine time has stopped, giving us the opportunity to look at it more closely.

Still images may be created by small groups, or by the whole group. They may be created quickly in the count to five, or they may be built one person at a time. This still image building approach enables children to respond to what others are doing in the still image by placing themselves in a position that relates to another's. A child seeing someone else in an image on a swing in a park may stand behind as though she is pushing the swing higher.

Storytelling

This series includes different modes of storytelling. Sometimes the teacher provides narration with pauses for the children to fill in. This involves them in the storytelling and makes their contribution part of the whole. At other times storytelling is suggested as a way to involve all the children in reviewing the events of the drama. Here each child takes it in turn to tell a line of the story. Older children can group into small circles to storytell together.

Teacher in role

The teacher takes the role of someone in the drama. This enables the teacher to work with the children from inside the drama. Additional information may be given through the teacher in role and questions can be posed to challenge the children's ideas and assumptions.

Thought tapping

Thought tapping is used in conjunction with mimed activity or most commonly with still images. Once the children are doing either of these, the teacher moves among them and taps them on the shoulder one at a time. She may ask about what they are doing, what they are thinking or feeling, or what they can see or smell or hear from where they are. It invites children to commit further to their roles and the drama, and to think more about the context. Their contributions become part of the shared understanding of the imaginary places and people. It is a quite controlled activity that gives less vocal individuals their moment.

Whole group improvisation

This activity involves the children and the teacher working together in role. The teacher will have teacher intentions in mind, but the ideas and suggestions offered by the children, and therefore the responses of the teacher, will vary when working with different groups. It is this mode of activity that often generates a high level of concentration and emotional commitment. Unlike dramatic play, the children are all engaged in one world, dealing with the same problem.

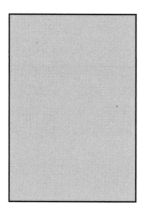

Suggestions for further reading

This is not a comprehensive list. There are many useful books available about drama in education and activities for the early years. We feel that the following books complement this series.

Ackroyd, J. (ed.) (2000) *Literacy Alive*, London: Hodder & Stoughton.

Ackroyd, J. and Boulton, J. (2001) *Drama Lessons for Five to Eleven-Year-Olds*, London: David Fulton.

Aldridge, M. (2003) *Meeting the Early Learning Goals through Role Play*, London: David Fulton.

Beetlestone, F. (1998) *Creative Children, Imaginative Teaching*, Buckingham: The Open University Press.

Bolton, G. (1984) *Drama as Education*, London: Longman.

Bolton, G. (1992) *New Perspectives on Classroom Drama*, London: Simon & Schuster Educational.

Booth, D. (1994) *Story Drama*, Markham: Pembroke.

Booth, D. (2002) *Even Hockey Players Read*, Markham: Pembroke.

Bowell, P. and Heap, B. (2001) *Planning Process Drama*, London: David Fulton.

Clipson-Boyles, S. (1999) *Drama in the Primary Classroom*, London: David Fulton.

Drake, J. (2003) *Organising Play in the Early Years*, London: David Fulton.

Emblen, V. and Helen, S. (1992) *Learning Through Story*, Leamington Spa: Scholastic.

Fleming, M. (1994) *Starting Drama Teaching*, London: David Fulton.

Kempe, A. and Holroyd, J. (2003) *Speaking, Listening and Drama*, London: David Fulton.

Miller, C. and Saxton, J. (2004) *Into the Story: Language in Action Through Drama*, New Hampshire: Heinemann.

Mudd, S. and Mason, H. (1993) *Tales for Topics: Linking Favourite Stories with Popular Topics for Children Aged Five to Nine*, Twickenham: Belair.

Neelands, J. (1992) *Learning Through Imagined Experience*, London: Hodder & Stoughton.

Neelands, J. and Goode, T. (2000) *Structuring Drama Work* (2nd edn), London: Hodder & Stoughton.

O'Neill, C. (1995) *Drama Worlds*, London: Heinemann.

Toye, N. and Prendiville, F. (2000) *Drama and Traditional Story for the Early Years*, London: Routledge/Falmer.

Winston, J. (2000) *Drama, Literacy and Moral Education 5–11*, London: David Fulton.

Winston, J. and Tandy, M. (2002) *Beginning Drama*, London: David Fulton.